MW00425974

"Mitri Raheb's *The Politics of Persecution* offers a trove of information and analysis for any Christians fascinated by the Holy Land and its neighbors. But beyond this, it will be of great interest to general readers of all kinds, basically for anyone interested in the emergence of the Modern Middle East. Raheb addresses many topics and issues that are presently barely known to nonspecialists, and he does a real service in describing so many of these episodes in lucid and approachable terms. *The Politics of Persecution* is ambitious in scope, thoroughly researched, and amply deserving of a wide readership."
—**Philip Jenkins**, *Distinguished Professor of History, Baylor University*

"Rev. Mitri Raheb's book goes deep in our collective historical consciousness. Those who made research on the persecution of Christians and the atrocities, massacres, and confiscation of wealth that they have been through understand better his concerns. Linking persecution to the different dimensions of our existence helps us see the broader scenery that led to what we have been experiencing for centuries and which is being accelerated with the changes that occur in the world order and the game of nations. This book puts before us a challenge by highlighting the reality that preserving our presence and safeguarding our dignity in the cradle of Christianity requires unprecedented approaches and a renewed role which we are called to define. While this book has been 'written by a native Palestinian Christian theologian who has spent his entire life in the region and is committed to continue living here,' this endorsement is written by a native Levantine Christian from Beirut who almost never left the area, who is keen on remaining on his land, and who has been always preaching this to his children as well as to his students. Rev. Dr. Mitri Raheb opens, through his book, and without even having met me, a dialogue with my very being."
—**Michel E. Abs**, *Secretary General, The Middle East Council of Churches*

"*The Politics of Persecution* is an outstanding demystification of the history of Middle East Christians under imperialism. Mitri Raheb offers an erudite study that exposes the pernicious dead ends of Western hegemonic discourses and practices. By employing thoughtful decolonial lenses, he convincingly repositions Middle Eastern Christians in networks of local and regional struggles that open the door for groundbreaking transnational solidarities. This is a must-read by anyone interested in decolonial studies, liberation theologies, Palestine/Israel, conflict and peace studies, interreligious conversations, and global struggles for justice."
—**Santiago Slabodsky**, *Florence and Robert Kaufman Chair in Jewish Studies, Hofstra University–New York*

"Raheb's new book offers a fresh approach to Christianity in the modern Middle East and an urgently needed challenge to portrayals of Middle Eastern Christians as passive victims of religious persecution. In mapping the geopolitical and demographic shifts in the region over the past two centuries, *The Politics of Persecution* links such simplistic persecution narratives to colonialist agendas. This rich study gives careful attention to the national, ethno-linguistic, denominational, and interreligious contexts within which Middle Eastern Christians have responded to these complex changes. Raheb invites students, researchers, and Christian readers in the West to listen to the voices of Middle Eastern Christians and celebrate their communities' resilience."
—**Deanna Ferree Womack**, *Assistant Professor of History of Religions and Multifaith Relations, Candler School of Theology, Emory University*

"In *The Politics of Persecution*, Mitri Raheb persuasively demonstrates how the language of 'persecution' has been selectively employed over the past century by Western imperial powers to justify both colonial interventions in the 19th and 20th centuries and contemporary incursions here in the 21st in the MENA region. He argues that both have created vs. mitigated political and social instabilities that are too often simplistically rendered as narrowly sectarian; where 'religious minorities' are 'persecuted' and in need of saving by the very Western powers that created the instability in the first place. His particular focus is Arab Christians, and he counters the portrayal of them as victims with a fulsome and rich representation of Arab Christians as diverse, creative, and resilient. This is a timely, concise, and accessible volume that should be widely read by those concerned with 'religious freedom' in the MENA region."
—**Diane L. Moore**, *Faculty Director of Religion and Public Life and Lecturer on Religion, Conflict, and Peace, Harvard Divinity School*

"Dr. Mitri Raheb is a pastor, university president, community developer, author, and as this volume demonstrates, he is also a compelling scholar. This book provides a historical analysis of the church in the Middle East in response to the relentless political and ecclesiastical agendas in the region. As he convincingly argues, the story of the Middle Eastern church is a compelling testimony of resilience."
—**M. Craig Barnes**, *President, Princeton Theological Seminary*

"Raheb touches upon a critical theme in the geopolitics of the Middle East: the persecution of Christians. While tracing the development of the Christian Community under the *Millet* system of the Ottoman Empire and chronicling the Massacre at Mount Lebanon and the Armenian Genocide, he argues that this notion is a 'western construct' used as a pretext by colonial powers in Europe and the United States to promote their interest in the region. Sustained by an Orientalist view of the region and its people, this construct has had a nefarious consequence for the Middle East: 'the instrumentalization of religion for socio-political gain.'"
—**Rafael Malpica Padilla**, *Executive Director, Service and Justice, Evangelical Lutheran Church in America*

"Mitri Raheb, a Palestinian theological master of our era, examines critically and through a timely decolonial lens the predicament of Middle Eastern Christians in the age of empire. Mitri's book is an act of revolutionary love, walking Jesus' path, and navigating the painful, complex resilience of Christian communities in the most difficult period in the region's history and Palestine in particular. The book is a must-read for anyone wanting to delve into the multifaceted history, appreciate the depth of coverage, and engage Middle Eastern Christians dialoguing from within their unique epistemology and lived experiences. Middle Eastern Christians speaking for themselves about themselves and the world is the foundation of Mitri's book, which is more needed in the age of empire than at any other time. A spiritual light and a message of hope from the heart of Bethlehem."
—**Hatem Bazian**, *Teaching Professor in the Departments of Near Eastern and Ethnic Studies at the University of California, Berkeley, and co-founder, Zaytuna College*

THE POLITICS OF PERSECUTION

MIDDLE EASTERN CHRISTIANS IN AN AGE OF EMPIRE

Mitri Raheb

BAYLOR UNIVERSITY PRESS

CONTENTS

ACKNOWLEDGMENTS

This book was developed out of research conducted on Middle Eastern Christianity in modern history between 2014 and 2019 during my time as the chairman of the Christian Academic Forum for Citizenship in the Arab World. In 2019, during a meeting with an American friend in Chicago, he asked me whether I could publish a book on the issue of Christian persecution in the Middle East that was well researched yet written for the general public. I took that to heart and promised him to work on it as my time allowed. The COVID-19 pandemic and the total lockdown on Bethlehem for months gave me the time to do the necessary research for this book.

I am grateful for Mark Sweeney, who encouraged me to write this book and who was instrumental in finding the right publisher.

I would like to acknowledge with gratitude the support of Elias Cade Jarrell, managing editor at Baylor University Press, and his colleagues for showing confidence in my work.

I would like to include a special note of thanks to Karen Mann, who edited the first draft and provided helpful comments, and for Hiba Nasser Atrash for her valuable assistance throughout the project. I would like also to thank my colleagues at Dar al-Kalima University library; the director, Anan Hamad; and Susan Gharib for the help provided during my research.

Finally, I would like to express my gratitude to my wife, Najwa, and to my daughters, Dana and Tala, who continue to provide the needed space, time, and moral support, especially as we continue to face a double lockdown caused by the pandemic and by the continuous Israeli occupation.

INTRODUCTION

Christian persecution as the systemic mistreatment of an individual Christian or a Christian community by another individual or group, based on their religious beliefs, is not a new phenomenon. It is a recurring biblical theme, referred to first during the Sermon on the Mount. In the Beatitudes, we hear Jesus saying: "Blessed are those who are persecuted because of righteousness, for theirs is the kingdom of heaven. Blessed are you when people insult you, persecute you and falsely say all kinds of evil against you because of me. Rejoice and be glad, because great is your reward in heaven, for in the same way they persecuted the prophets who were before you" (Matt 5:10-12). Several books in the New Testament—the Letter to the Hebrews or the book of Revelation—were addressed to persecuted Christian communities. The first three centuries were marked by periodical Christian persecution under Roman emperors from Nero to Trajan, Decius, Valerian, and all the way to Diocletian.

Persecution was perceived as an important characteristic of the early church in the Middle East. As a Middle Eastern Christian, I grew up surrounded by stories of the many martyrs who are venerated in the Eastern Churches as saints: the first New Testament martyr, Stephen (Acts 7); James, son of Zebedee (Acts 12); Justin the martyr from Nablus and the Forty Martyrs of Sebaste; and the female Palestinian saint, Barbara. All of these were martyrs of the early church in Palestine. As a Lutheran, I was also familiar with Protestant martyrs like the Czech martyr John Hus and the first Middle Eastern Protestant martyr, As'ad Shidyaq. These were all stories from the past that we admired, but no more than that.

1

In the mid-1990s, the issue of Christian persecution became more and more problematic for me. Following the signing of the Oslo Agreement between Israel and the Palestinian Liberation Organization (PLO) in 1993, Israel was to withdraw from specific occupied areas in the West Bank, known as Area A, and to hand these areas over to the newly established Palestinian Authority under Chairman Arafat. By Christmas 1995, Bethlehem, the city where I live and work, was under Palestinian rule. For us as Palestinian Christians, this was a time for celebration, liberation from Israeli military occupation, and a first step toward independence and statehood. Yet, this was not the story the Western media was interested in. The majority of journalists who have interviewed me since then wanted to hear about Christian persecution under Palestinian (and Muslim) rule. They were not really interested in our views but simply sought the sound bite they wanted to use. They wanted us to say that we are persecuted. The fact that Christians are an integral part of the Palestinian people as a whole and that our biggest threat is the Israeli occupation of our land and livelihood was not what they wanted to hear. Numerous articles published by Western and Israeli journalists over the past twenty-five years depict Palestinian Christians as victims persecuted by the Palestinian Authority. Unfortunately, a small number of Palestinian Christians earn their livelihood by disseminating such misinformation. With the exception of mainly Catholic press agencies, I also noticed that very few news outlets have covered the recurring attacks conducted by Jewish extremist groups on churches inside Israel. My encounters with many journalists have highlighted the importance of applying the hermeneutics of suspicion when dealing with the discourse of Christian persecution. It also triggered interest in research into the politics behind this discourse.

Over the past decade, I have investigated the status of Christians in the Middle East, and specifically the relationship between religion and state in the region. To that end, a program was introduced at Dar al-Kalima University of Arts and Culture, a higher education institute that I founded in 2006 and continue to lead, to study the situation of Christians in six Middle Eastern countries:

Egypt, Palestine, Israel, Lebanon, Jordan, and Syria. This program led to the establishment of the Christian Academic Forum for Citizenship in the Arab World. We have conducted many regional workshops and conferences and published several books. I would like to highlight one of them: *Shifting Identities: Changes in the Social, Political, and Religious Structures in the Middle East.*[1] While my previous works focused mainly on Palestine, through this program I was intrigued to look at the larger regional scene, and this is an important feature of the book. Rather than focusing on the situation of one country per se, a region-wide lens proved important to identify overarching themes, cross-cutting issues, and geopolitical tectonic changes. The regional approach is also an important tool to depict contrasts and the unique features of each context.

In line with my approach in *Faith in the Face of Empire: The Bible through Palestinian Eyes,*[2] I also chose to look at the issue of Christian persecution from a geopolitical perspective. This book will therefore examine the geopolitical tectonic shifts that took place, starting with the Ottoman era and covering French and British rule, the eras of independence, pan-Arabism and pan-Islamism, and the current era of the American Empire (hence the subtitle *Middle Eastern Christians in the Age of Empire*). What distinguishes this book from others is the fact that it places the status of Christians within the wider geopolitical context of the Middle East. It looks at how international factors and regional developments have affected the presence of Christians in this region, the rise and fall of Middle Eastern Christianity, and the role played by Christians during different eras.

Rather than focusing on one specific period of history, I chose to examine the situation of Christians of the Middle East over two centuries, from the invasion of Napoleon Bonaparte in 1799 to the so-called Arab Spring. This longue durée approach offers a more substantive understanding of the history with all of its ups and downs. As a church historian, I view history as a dynamic and fluid process that needs constant reinterpretation rather than a static collection of chronological events or facts. In this book I provide an alternative interpretation of the history of Middle Eastern Christianity.

The issue of Christian persecution has undergone a resurgence since the election of President Donald Trump and has, once again, become a tool of international diplomacy. Middle Eastern Christians have often been orientalized, victimized, and minoritized. Many people in the West claim to speak on their behalf. An important and unique feature of this book is that it is written by a native Palestinian Christian theologian who has spent his entire life in the region and is committed to continue living here. As such, it provides a decolonial interpretation, a perspective from the inside rather than an external hegemonic and colonial perspective. This perspective allows us to expose the orientalist perception dominant in Western discourse. Often, history is dictated and written by those in power, it is *his*-story, their version of the story. This book offers an alternative version of our story as we see and experience it. The days when Western forces claimed a mandate over us on the grounds that we were not ready to assume leadership are over. Now it is time for us to speak on our own, to tell our story, and to resist all attempts to turn us into objects.

This book builds on many contributions and research projects conducted over the past twenty years. There has been renewed interest in the status of the Christians of the Middle East by renowned historians and scholars. While there is no way to mention all of them, I would like to name the following people. I am indebted to the foundational works of Usama Makdisi on *The Culture of Sectarianism*[3] and *Age of Coexistence*.[4] Makdisi's work focuses on Lebanon. For Palestine, the work of Rashid Khalidi, especially his latest, *The Hundred Years' War on Palestine*,[5] is groundbreaking. Laura Robson's publications *Minorities in the Arab World*[6] and *States of Separation: Transfer, Partition and the Making of the Modern Middle East*[7] are important contributions to the field. Last but not least, the research of Heather Sharkey on Egypt and Sudan, and especially her book *A History of Muslims, Christians, and Jews in the Middle East*,[8] provides an important addition to the modern history of Middle Eastern Christianity.

I had the pleasure of working with Mark Lamport on a major work on Middle Eastern Christianity that was released recently: the Rowman and Littlefield *Handbook of Christianity in the Middle*

East, a handbook covering the history of Middle Eastern Christianity over twenty centuries, with contributions by fifty of the top scholars in the field. Together with Mark Lamport, I am editing another volume, to be published by Cascade Books under the title *Surviving Jewel: An Enduring Story of Christianity in the Middle East*, with contributions by another twenty distinguished scholars. These two volumes tell the story of Middle Eastern Christianity over the past twenty centuries. I chose here to focus on only the past two centuries since this is the area of my expertise, having written my dissertation on the history of the Lutheran Church in Palestine in modern history.

The book is divided into twelve chapters that chart the major geopolitical changes that took place in the region during the past two centuries.

Chapter 1, "Under Ottoman Rule," gives a clear overview of the socioeconomic and religious status of Christians in the nineteenth-century Ottoman Empire, and the major shift that was brought about by the rise of Muhammad Ali and the Ottoman reforms that followed.

Chapter 2, "Religious Mobility," looks at European penetration into the Ottoman Empire, which coincided with the arrival of Protestant and Catholic missionaries in the Middle East. Those missions, which came originally to convert Jews and Muslims or to bind the oriental churches to Rome, ended up creating local congregations from the Eastern Churches.

Chapter 3, "A Massacre on Mount Lebanon," analyses the socioeconomic changes that took place in conjunction with Ottoman reform. It discusses the emerging culture of sectarianism that led to a civil war between the Druze and the Christian communities that ended with a Christian massacre on Mount Lebanon. The narrative of sectarianism was opposed by local Christian intellectuals who advocated an alternative paradigm based on a civic framework of coexistence.

Chapter 4, "Agents of Renaissance," looks at the major changes brought about by Christian schools, the printing press, a literary revival, and the role played by Christians in the second half of the nineteenth century. The penetration by European powers had disastrous consequences for the region by introducing Zionism, nationalism, and colonialism.

Chapter 5, "Christian Zionism," analyzes the rise of Christian sectarian perspectives in Britain that weaponized theology and employed politics to convert Jews to Christianity. Jews were then used as subcontractor settlers for British interests in Palestine, thus paving the way for the creation of a Jewish homeland there.

Chapter 6, "The Road to Genocide," highlights the role of colonial powers in supporting ethnoreligious nationalism to weaken the Ottoman Empire. The empire's response of religious Turkish nationalism led ultimately to the Assyrian and Armenian Genocide, with the passive involvement of the Germans.

Chapter 7, "Minorities in Nation-States," analyzes how between the two world wars, the European powers portrayed Christians as minorities who required protection. This era was marked by a Christian quest for both national and ecclesiastical independence.

Chapter 8, "A Catastrophe," looks at the plight of the Palestinian Christians following the 1948 War that led to the displacement of over one-third of the Palestinian Christian community and to further migration in the following decades.

Chapter 9, "Arab and Christian," looks at the impact of pan-Arab ideology and politics on the Christians of the Middle East and their search for independence and unity, as well as the impact of nationalization on their ministries.

Chapter 10, "A Turning Point," studies the ramifications of the 1967 War on the region and on Christians. Special attention is given to the rise of Jewish messianism, Islamic fundamentalism, and Christian Zionism.

Chapter 11, "Petrodollars," examines the role of the 1973 October War. It charts the rise of Iran and Saudi Arabia, the influence of the petrodollar in triggering a wave of Islamization, followed by the so-called Arab Spring, ISIS (Islamic State), and the effects on Middle Eastern Christianity.

Chapter 12, "Challenging Times," examines the key challenges facing the whole Middle East region in the twenty-first century and the consequences for the Christians of the region.

The epilogue looks at the approach of the Trump administration and the use of freedom of religion as a tool for international diplomacy. The epilogue summarizes the main findings of the study and highlights the history of Middle Eastern Christians as one of resilience rather than persecution.

My hope is that this book, written for a wider audience, will offer an alternative reading of the story and history of Middle Eastern Christians, and will deepen the renewed interest in a region that continues to be in the eye of imperial storms.

1

UNDER OTTOMAN RULE

The year 1516/17 marked a new phase in the history of West Asia and North Africa (or what later came to be called the Middle East). In the same year that Martin Luther posted his ninety-five theses on the doors of the church in Wittenberg, triggering the whole process that led to the Reformation, new invaders known as the Ottomans came to occupy larger Syria (what is today Syria, Lebanon, Jordan, Israel, and Palestine), Egypt, and parts of Libya and Saudi Arabia. The Ottomans were a tribe that emerged in northwestern Anatolia (Turkey today) around 1299 and over a century expanded their territory throughout Asia Minor (Turkey today). In 1453 they conquered Constantinople, ending the era of the Byzantine Empire and rising to becoming the major power of the region. By the early nineteenth century, the Ottoman Empire stretched over three continents: from Libya in North Africa to Iraq in Asia, including Greater Syria, and from the Balkans in Europe to Yemen on the Red Sea.

The Ottoman Empire became the successor of the Roman Empire not only in terms of geography but also modus operandi. The Ottoman Empire was the most diverse multiethnic, multilingual and multireligious entity of its time. In the sixteenth century, Christians may have constituted about 7 percent of the total population of the Middle East.[1] Yet the Christians represented the most diverse religion in the empire.

In the early nineteenth century, there were three groupings of churches in the Middle East. The first such grouping may be described as "national churches"; these were the remnants of ancient Christian "ethno-cultural" communities. Within these, cultural identity, religious heritage, language, and geography formed a unity. This was the case for the Coptic Orthodox Church of Alexandria in Egypt; the Syriac Orthodox Church (also known as the Syrian Orthodox Church of Antioch) based in Syria, Iraq, and Turkey; and the Armenian Apostolic Church located beside Asia Minor, mainly in northern Syria. These three church bodies belong to the Oriental Orthodox family and are also known as miaphysite or non-Chalcedonian churches. To this grouping, though distinct, also belongs the Assyrian Church of the East in Mesopotamia, Iran, and Turkey (previously called Nestorians).

The second grouping of church bodies consisted of the three "Greek Orthodox" patriarchates: the Greek Orthodox patriarchate of Jerusalem, the Greek Orthodox patriarchate of Antioch and All the East, and the Greek Orthodox Church of Alexandria and All Africa. Along with the Ecumenical Patriarchate of Constantinople, these churches are remnants of the ancient Byzantine Empire and are also known as Rum Orthodox, *rum* being an Arabic term implying "Byzantine."

A third grouping of oriental churches was that of the Oriental Catholic churches, today commonly called Eastern Catholic Churches. To this category belonged the Greek Melkite Catholic Patriarchates of Antioch, Alexandria, and Jerusalem; the Armenian Catholic Church; the Syrian Catholic Church of Antioch; the Coptic Catholic Church; and the Chaldean Catholic Church. These churches, each with its own distinctive history, entered into full communion with the Roman Catholic Church. While they were able to maintain their oriental liturgies and ecclesiastical languages, they recognized the pope of Rome as their supreme head. By the early nineteenth century, most of these churches were not yet officially recognized by the Ottomans but were nevertheless conducting services and programs.

In addition to these church bodies, there were the Franciscans, who came to the Holy Land as early as 1217 and were directed by Pope Gregory IX to serve as custodians of churches and shrines. From there, the Franciscans spread to Beirut in the mid-fourteenth century and later to Aleppo, Tripoli, and Damascus.

By the early nineteenth century, Arabic was the lingua franca of the majority of the Christians of the region. While some Christians might have been fluent in Turkish, the language of the empire, Turkish was never the language of the people of West Asia / North Africa. This resulted from the tolerant Ottoman policy that gave the occupied peoples the right to continue using and cultivating their own language and culture without interference from the central government. Arabic was the main language for the Orthodox Christians of Greater Syria and Coptic Christians of Egypt. In some remote areas in the eastern provinces of the empire, Syriac and Assyrian Christians continued to use Aramaic, while Armenians in Aleppo were communicating in their native Armenian language. However, all of the Christians of the region continued to cultivate their ancient liturgical languages. Church services were conducted in Greek for the Orthodox; in Coptic for the Copts; in Aramaic for the Maronites, Syriac, and Chaldeans; in Armenian for the Armenians; and in Latin for the churches supported by the Franciscans.

The relationship between these churches and the Ottoman Empire was regulated by the so-called millet system. The term "millet" implied a "national or ethnic community" that was associated with a particular religion. These communities or denominations were headed by a patriarch or bishop and were given a certain autonomy to handle their own religious and social affairs, as long as they accepted the political supremacy of the Muslim Ottoman Empire. Recognized millets were given the right to have their own legal courts to manage all personal status laws such as marriage and inheritance. In a sense they were a kind of "ecclesiastical state" without any political claims since they functioned within the framework of the Ottoman Empire, headed by the sultan who claimed the title of "caliph" (successor of the Prophet Mohammed).

Two of these denominations within the millet system had the closest ties to the Ottoman authorities: both the Greek Orthodox and the Armenian Churches had their patriarchs in Istanbul and thus had direct access to the sultan's palace. In turn, the sultans had their own interest in consolidating church affairs in the hands of patriarchs who were in close proximity to the palace and thereby under their direct control. However, this church-state arrangement was not a static, centralized, and rigid system but took the form of a series of arrangements that varied according to the context. The situation of Christians fluctuated over time and from one location to another. Although Christians were not equal to Muslims, the system provided them with political protection. Besides the protection offered by the Ottoman Empire itself, two other empires claimed the rights to protect Christians living within Ottoman domains. France claimed the right to protect Roman Catholic Christians and those communions united with the Church of Rome. Following the Treaty of Kuchuk Kainarja (Bulgaria, 1774) between the Ottoman and Russian Empires, the Russian Orthodox Church also claimed the right to protect Orthodox Christians.

Within the church-state relationship, Muslims ran the state and the military exclusively. In lieu of military service, Christians had to pay a special per capita tax called *jizya*. While Muslims ran the government, state, and army, Christians operated a substantial portion of the empire's economy. The socioeconomic situation of the Christians varied widely from one country to another. In Egypt, the largest concentration of Coptic Christians lived in Upper Egypt where Christians were mainly farmers involved in diverse agricultural activities along the Nile. Cities like Assiut, Cairo, and Alexandria also had large Christian populations. The Copts played an important administrative role in Egyptian financial institutions in areas such as tax collection, money exchange, and customs. In Syria-Lebanon, the majority of Maronites lived in villages in the mountains of Lebanon and the Kadisha Valley. While there were many Christian farmers in Syria, Iraq, and Palestine, large numbers of Christians also lived in towns and cities such as Damascus, Aleppo, Baghdad, Mosul, Jerusalem, Bethlehem, and Nazareth. Most Greek Orthodox Christians were found along the Mediterranean shore in cities such as Alexandria, Jaffa, Beirut, and Tripoli. Many of the Christians living in these cities were merchants with already existing ties to Europe and its commerce. A large number of the Christians throughout the region were craftspeople, as reflected in many Arab Christian family names: Najjar (carpenter),

Khayyat and Tarazi (tailor), Bustani (gardener), Lahham (butcher), Qattan (one who work with cotton), Sarraf (tax collector / money exchange), and so on. Working with metals, including precious metals, was an almost exclusively Christian profession and was reflected in the names Sayigh or Gawahri (jeweler) and Haddad (smith). This meant that the socioeconomic situation of Christians was relatively good, and they were often better off financially than their Muslim neighbors. However, the heavy taxes paid by Christians, which created a substantial revenue for the empire treasury, sometimes led Christians to convert to Islam as an avoidance mechanism. Socially speaking, Christians lived largely separated from Muslims, either in Christian quarters, villages, or city sections around their churches. Nevertheless, there were many mixed villages and neighborhoods, in addition to daily points of contacts in the public sphere and in areas like agriculture, trade, and administration.

The system exercised by the Ottomans gave the Christians wider autonomy and authority than that they had previously during the Byzantine Empire. This autonomy was not so much a favor of the Ottomans to the Christians but a deliberate policy to maintain the empire's unity and stability. Indeed, this stability lasted for three centuries. By the early nineteenth century, the great Ottoman Empire had become known as the "sick man of the Bosphorus." The year that Napoleon landed in Egypt, 1798, conventionally marks the beginning of the end of the Ottoman Empire. The arrival of Napoleon on Egyptian soil signaled a new era of European intervention despite the fact that he was forced to leave after three years.

However, the major change to the empire did not come from Napoleon but from inside the empire, triggered by Muhammad Ali Pasha (1769–1849), an Ottoman Albanian who seized power over Egypt after the withdrawal of Napoleon. By 1811 Muhammad Ali was able to end the reign of the Mamluks in Egypt, who were functioning as subcontractors to the Ottomans. After seizing power in Egypt, Muhammad Ali went on to occupy the Hijaz region (a region of Saudi Arabia along the Red Sea) in 1812 and the Sudan in 1821. His dream was to create a modern mega-state on a European model that would cover the area between the Nile and the Euphrates. Toward that goal, his son Ibrahim occupied large parts of Syria, including Palestine, in 1831. This move presented a threat not only to the Ottoman rulers but also to Europeans whose interests in the Middle East were crucial, particularly England and Austria. For those European powers it was better to deal with a sick empire than with the unknown. In order to ensure control of trade routes and resources, these countries mobilized their forces and brought about the withdrawal of Ibrahim Pasha from the territory of Greater Syria. From that point in time, the dynasty of Muhammad Ali was to control Egypt, leading it into modernity. Muhammad Ali created a modern military force and brought about major economic, cultural, and religious reforms.

By the early 1830s the millet system that treated Christians as "separate, unequal, and protected" had to change, slowly but surely. Muhammad Ali's concept was to build a national state based on equal citizenship that was distinct from the Ottoman Empire based on religious affiliation. In 1832 Muhammad Ali declared his concept: "Muslims and Christians are all our subjects. The question of religion is not linked to political considerations. [In religious matters] every individual must be left free: the believer to practice his Islam and the Christian his Christianity. But no one is to have authority over the other."[2] This was Muhammad Ali's version of the modern national state that separates state from religion and confines religion to the private sphere. During the era of Muhammad Ali, European and American consulates were opened in major cities of the Middle East such as Alexandria, Damascus, Beirut, and Jerusalem. Missionaries were able to work freely. "The Christian missionary enjoys perfect liberty to carry on his operations under the Egyptian government, more so indeed than under the British government at Malta or India."[3]

The rise of Muhammad Ali forced the Ottomans to stabilize their internal rule and to modernize their military apparatus. In return for the European powers forcing Muhammad Ali and his son, Ibrahim Pasha, to leave Syria and Palestine, the Ottomans had to make concessions and introduced major political and administrative reforms. In 1839 the Edict of Gühane was signed by Sultan Abdulmecid I and started an era of reforms known as the Tanzimat[4] (literally, "reorganization") that guaranteed, among other things, the rights of Ottoman citizens irrespective of religion or race. Such rights were becoming urgent, especially in light of the Greek withdrawal from the empire in 1832 to establish an independent monarchy; there was also rising dissatisfaction among other Eastern European communities within the empire. Following the Crimean War and the intervention of Britain and France in support of the Ottoman Empire against Russia, a new imperial decree known as Hatti Humayun, an official Edict of Reform of the Ottoman government, was propagated in 1856. This edict initiated further reforms including freedom of worship, the ability to maintain and repair church properties, the right to open schools, and the right of foreigners to acquire land. These Ottoman reforms reflect an increasing European influence that opened the door for Western Catholic and Protestant missions to arrive in the Middle East, disturb the static millet system, and create religious mobility that consequently led to greater Christian visibility.

2

RELIGIOUS MOBILITY

The era of Muhammad Ali brought major changes to the Middle East, one of which was religious mobility. Muhammad Ali allowed foreign missionaries to work freely in the areas under his control. However, the missionaries were very few in number and were mainly traveling missionaries who moved between cities to debate about religion. This changed in 1858 when the Ottoman government made reforms that allowed foreigners to buy and own land. This new legislation opened the door for missionary organizations to think of establishing permanent "mission stations" in the region. The establishment of mission stations went hand in hand with the opening of foreign embassies. European intervention in the Middle East in the mid-nineteenth century was not only political and military in nature, but also sociocultural, economic, and religious, through the missionary agencies.

The Catholic European mission to the Middle East started at the time of the Crusades. The Franciscans arrived in the Holy Land following the Fourth Crusade. However, for several centuries they remained the only European Christian order. Several attempts were made to establish Catholic orders in Lebanon but without much success. Two factors played an important role in a renewed Catholic mission to the Middle East. The first was the establishment of the Congregation for the Propagation of the Faith in 1622. The second was the Capitulations Agreement between France and the Ottoman Empire (1569, 1604, and 1740). The Capuchins were the first to arrive and settle in Aleppo in 1623. After obtaining official permission from the Sublime Porte, they spread quickly to Cyprus, Egypt, Lebanon, Syria, and Iraq.[1] The Jesuits arrived in Aleppo in 1625 but could not start their mission officially until the mid-seventeenth century. Their initial mission was to care for the spiritual needs of the European merchants in the coastal towns in Lebanon. Later they engaged in the fields of education, translation, and health care for the Maronite Christians. In 1632 the Carmelites came and settled on Mount Carmel in Palestine, from where they then spread into Iraq and Iran. The Lazarist Fathers arrived in 1763 in Jerusalem and Antioch.

> The task of the first Catholic missions to the Middle Eastern countries involved relinking the Middle Eastern Churches to Rome through reform and renewal. This Rome-inspired undertaking aimed at going beyond mere union at the top and seeking a base so as to educate believers and organize the parish "according to an ideal delineated in Catholic Europe." Undoubtedly the missions as a whole were the spearhead of Rome's program in leading many of the adherents of the Middle Eastern churches to form new churches that declared their clear allegiance to the papacy.[2]

However, by the early nineteenth century the Catholic orders in the Middle East were either too weak or nonexistent. The French revolution with its anti-Catholic and anti-papal policies had taken its toll on the French Catholic Church and its many orders.

Simultaneously with these developments in Catholic France, major changes were taking place within the Protestant landscape in Europe and the United States. Following a series of religious revivals in Germany and England in the eighteenth century, a second religious revival, known as the Second Great Awakening, started in New England and swept through the United States (ca. 1790–1850). The nineteenth century was to become the century of Christian mission and the largest mission expansion in history. The rationale behind this mainly Protestant movement was that every Christian has an obligation to actively participate in the conversion of the "heathens," those who were not yet touched in any way by the gospel or Christian civilization. It was in this context that the Protestant mission arrived in the Middle East, though there were no heathens in the eras of occupation by the Ottoman Empire. On the contrary, Palestine and Greater Syria are the cradle of Christianity. The population of the Ottoman Empire was majority Muslim, a good percentage of Christians, and a Jewish minority, all members of the three monotheistic religions.

The rationale behind the mission to the Middle East region was best expressed in two sermons given by the first two missionaries recruited by the American Board of Commissioners for Foreign Missions, a congregational mission agency established in Massachusetts in 1810. Pliny Fisk and Levi Parsons were recruited to go to Palestine and establish a mission station, preferably in Jerusalem or else in Bethlehem. Both missionaries were aware that their mission there was different than that to the "heathens." Pliny Fisk made that very clear in his sermon:

> All the inhabitants of the country believe in one God, and the leading facts recorded in the Old Testament. Here are no gods of brass or wood; no temples to Juggernaut, or the Grand Lama; no funeral piles; no altars stained with the blood of human victims. Everywhere you see a faint glimmering of light, through the gross and almost impenetrable darkness.

Then he added:

> These people are not sunk in such entire stupidity and such brutal ignorance, as are the Hindoos of India, and the Hottentots of Africa. Here is intellect, enterprise, and some degree of literature and science. Here several classes of men are among the most interesting that dwell on earth and are worthy of the prayers and the attentions of all those who desire to see influence, learning, talent, and strength of character consecrated to Christ.[3]

Yet all of these attributes were not good enough. Pliny Fisk and Levi Parsons were convinced that they were called for a much more important and noble task. They shared the millennialist conviction that four developments were necessary for the second coming of Christ: the revival of the oriental churches, the conversion of Muslims to Christ, the defeat of the pope, and the restoration of the Jews.[4] So their mission was clear: to revive the churches of the Orient, to convert Jews and Muslims, and to do this before and better than the Roman Catholics. These four features were, to varying degrees, the main characteristics of Protestant missions to the nineteenth-century Ottoman Empire.

Before the arrival of the two American missionaries in 1819, the London Missionary Society, which had been established in 1795, sent a missionary to Malta in 1808 in order "to reawaken the pure religion in the Greek Orthodox Church."[5] In Malta the same society established a publication house for the printing and distribution of Bibles and Christian literature. In the same year the London Society for Promoting Christianity amongst the Jewish People, widely known as the London Jews Society, was established to relieve "the temporal distress of the Jews and the promotion of their welfare."[6] In 1839, and only after the occupation of Palestine by Ibrahim Pasha, was it possible for this mission organization to break ground for the first Protestant church building in the Ottoman Empire. This was the achievement of John Nicolayson (or Hans Nicolajsen, 1803–1856), a missionary of the London Jews Society. Interestingly enough, this church was located in the Armenian Quarter of the Old City of Jerusalem, where it is still standing.

While missionaries concentrated on the conversion of Jews and Muslims, European politicians had other ambitions. Following the defeat of Muhammad Ali and the realization that the Ottoman Empire was close to disintegrating, the European countries entered into a debate about the future of Palestine, the Holy Land. In the same year that Ibrahim Pasha, Muhammad Ali's son, was pushed back out of Syria (1940), Friedrich Wilhelm IV (1795–1861) became king of Prussia. The newly crowned king had his own ideas concerning Palestine. He first developed the idea of Palestine being in an extra-territorial setting, but after a week he developed the idea of the internationalization of Jerusalem and its surrounding area as a protectorate of the five principal European powers: England, Russia, Austria, France, and Prussia.[7] However, Prussia was a new player on the European stage and had little power, so this proposal was never taken seriously. A third proposal was feasible. The Prussian king was fully aware of the difficulties facing new converts to the Protestant faith since Protestantism was not recognized within the millet system of the Ottoman Empire. The king's goal was to obtain for Protestants already settled in Turkey, whether foreigners or Ottoman subjects, "securities and protection similar to those which Christians of other denominations enjoy."[8] He aimed at securing the recognition of Protestantism as a millet within the Ottoman Empire, and he was convinced that only a united Protestant church body could win this recognition. A Protestant millet would grant a protectorate over the Protestant Christians of England and Prussia similar to that of Russia over Orthodox Christians, and that of France over the Roman Catholics and Greek Catholic churches. Thus, Prussia would attain equal footing in the Holy Land and would allow the King at a future point to establish a German Protestant bishopric in Bethlehem.[9] To achieve these goals, Friedrich Wilhelm sent instructions to his personal envoy at the court of Queen Victoria, Christian Karl Josias, requesting the Church of England to establish a bishopric in Jerusalem in which a United (Lutheran-Reformed) Prussian Church could participate. This move was prompted by the desire of the Prussian king to establish a United Protestant Church and a bishopric system in Prussia. On July 19, 1841, an agreement was reached, signed on December 7 of that year, to establish in Jerusalem a "bishopric of the United Church of England and Ireland" and to send a bishop to Jerusalem who would be nominated alternately by the crowns of England and Prussia. Two days later a Statement of Proceeding for this agreement was published which indicated the duties of the bishop:

> His chief missionary care will be directed to the conversion of the Jews, to their protection, and to their useful employment. He will establish and maintain, as far as in him lies, relations of Christian charity with other churches represented at Jerusalem, and in particular with the Orthodox Greek Church; taking special care to convince them that the Church of England does not wish to disturb, or divide, or interfere with them; but that she is ready, in the spirit of Christian love, to render them such offices of friendship as they may be willing to receive.[10]

For the fulfillment of the mission laid out in the Statement of Proceeding, a Jewish convert was deemed the most capable. Accordingly, Professor Dr. Michael Solomon Alexander (1799–1845) was chosen as the first Anglican bishop of Jerusalem; he arrived there in January 1842. Bishop Alexander concentrated on the conversion of Jews. This proved to be a difficult task even for a converted Jew. By 1847 only fifty-seven Jews there had converted to Anglicanism.

On November 26, 1845, Bishop Alexander died, and the king of Prussia nominated Samuel Gobat (1799–1879)[11] to succeed him. Bishop Gobat shifted the emphasis from the conversion of Jews to the reformation of the oriental churches, a work for which he proved well suited. Soon after his arrival in Jerusalem on December 30, 1846, Bishop Gobat started the circulation of Bibles among members of the oriental churches. He introduced scripture reading by individuals as well as group Bible study, novel programs for the oriental churches for whom the Bible was mainly the book for the liturgy. Since most people were illiterate, he first opened Bible Schools where the scriptures were the main tool for teaching. By the time of his death in 1879, Bishop Gobat had established twelve Protestant congregations in the Holy Land. The polity of these congregations was in accord with Anglican structures where the bishop had final authority. In addition to building schools and establishing congregations, Bishop Gobat successfully endeavored to persuade German mission societies to take up work in Palestine: Kaiserswerther Diakonissen whose deaconesses concentrated on social ministry, health, and female education; Jerusalemsverein, which focused largely on the establishment of schools and supporting congregational work; and Schneller, which maintained an orphanage and a vocational school in Jerusalem. In a colonial manner, and to coordinate work between the German and English missionary societies, Bishop Gobat worked out a gentlemen's agreement between the two. Under this agreement, northern Palestine was to become the mission field for the English missionaries and southern Palestine was for the Germans. Largely as a consequence of this arrangement, Lutheran congregations are today found mainly south of Jerusalem while Anglican congregations lie chiefly in northern Palestine.

While British and German missions were somewhat successful in Palestine, the American missions were not. Although Levi
Parsons and Pliny Fisk were sent as missionaries to Jerusalem, for a
variety of reasons Beirut rather than Jerusalem became the American Protestant base for six missionaries sent by the American
Board: Levi Parsons, Pliny Fisk, Isaac Bird, Jonas King, Eli Smith,
and William Goodell, all graduates of the Andover Theological
Seminary. In 1827 a nucleus for the first Protestant congregation
in the Middle East came together, and with the first baptism conducted by the American missionaries, Middle Eastern Protestantism was born. Interestingly enough, the first child to be baptized
in the new church was not a Jew or a Muslim but the son of an
Armenian bishop, Dionysius Karapet. It took another twenty years
before the National Evangelical Church of Beirut was established
on March 31, 1848. The newly formed church body adopted Presbyterianism as its form of polity.[12] The American missionary Eli
Smith (1801–1857) was appointed pastor of the new congregation.
One of its prominent members was Butrus al-Bustani (1819–1883),
who was a candidate to become the first Arab Protestant pastor
in the Middle East, although he proved unready for such a step;
he later became a leading intellectual and a proponent of the
"Arab Renaissance," which began during the second half of the
nineteenth century. At the same time, the Protestants were recognized as an independent millet within the Ottoman Empire. Eli
Smith, in cooperation with Butrus al-Bustani and Nasif al-Yaziji
(1800–1871), a prominent Ottoman author, undertook to translate
the Bible into Arabic, a work completed in 1865 with the assistance
of Cornelius Van Dyck (1818–1895), an American medical missionary who gained a deep knowledge of the Arabic language and its
literature. This translation of the Bible was a major accomplish-
ment; it became a standard work and has been in use for over a
century among Middle East Protestants and also within the Coptic
Orthodox Church in Egypt.

While Anglican and Lutheran missions proved to be successful in Palestine, and Congregationalists successful in Lebanon,
the Presbyterians were the most successful in Egypt. Moravian
missionaries reached Egypt[13] during the eighteenth century. They

stayed in Cairo and the Middle Egypt for thirty years (1752–1782) without much success. In 1825 a different group of Protestant missionaries arrived in Egypt. These later missionaries were associated with the evangelical Anglican Church Mission Society (CMS). At that particular time the resources (funding and staff) of the CMS did not match the group's global ambitions, and its influence in Egypt was limited. It was the Presbyterians who succeeded in having the greatest impact in Egypt, becoming the largest Protestant church in the Middle East.

The first Presbyterian missionary arrived in Egypt with his wife in November 1850, representing Scottish-Irish Presbyterianism. The main aims of this mission were to reach out to Jews and Muslims with the basic Christian message and to reform the ancient Coptic Church. Work started in Lower Egypt: Cairo, Alexandria, and the Nile Delta. In May 1853, the General Synod of the Presbyterian Church in North America decided to send one of its missionaries operating in Syria to Egypt. Egypt proved to be fruitful ground for Presbyterianism. On September 15, 1859, a small group of four converts was accepted into the new Presbyterian church, including an Egyptian monk, a Syrian tradesperson, and an Armenian jewelry maker. As in Beirut and Jerusalem, the Armenians appeared to have been the group most open to Protestantism. On April 13, 1860, the first Egyptian Presbyterian Synod was organized, and in 1899 it included the Sudan, thus forming the "Synod of the Nile." On January 5, 1863, the first Presbyterian (at that time called Evangelical) congregation was formed officially in Cairo. That same year, a theological seminary was established, initially using a boat in which students received instruction while sailing up and down the Nile with their teachers to carry out evangelistic missions in the river villages. In 1871 the first indigenous Egyptian pastor was ordained. As the century came to a close, the Synod of the Nile experienced continuing maturity and growth with the establishment of schools, hospitals, development programs for self-governance, and social service projects.

Alongside North Africa and West Asia, several Protestant communities were established in Iraq by the British Church Mission Society as early as the first half of the nineteenth century. Armenian Presbyterians established churches in Baghdad, Mosul, Kirkuk, and Basra. In 1893 the National Evangelical Church in Bahrain became the first church to be started in the Gulf region.

Just as Muhammad Ali was able to challenge the policies and practices of the dominating Ottoman Empire, so the Protestant missions to the Middle East shook up the prevailing status quo among the local ancient churches. The missionaries thought of themselves as superior in religion, race, and culture to the other monotheistic religions as well as to the local churches. They often looked at them through the prism of orientalism.[14] No wonder that the reaction of those same ancient churches to the Protestant missionaries and their "new converts" was not at all welcoming.

The Protestant missionaries viewed the local Orthodox churches as "dead." Andrew Watson could describe the Egyptian Coptic Christians as "Christian in name, Christian in form, [it] was well typified by the mummified human body taken out of the tombs."[15] Often the liturgies of the ancient churches of the Middle East were characterized as sound without content, form without power, and bodies without a soul. It is understandable that the local churches would not stand by and accept these attacks, especially after some of their members started following the Protestants by conversion and leaving behind the faith of their ancestors. Thus, several of the ancient churches launched counterattacks. They accused the missionaries of being intruders, foreigners, "Englishmen," or heretics who had run away from the "Mother Church." Since the missionaries were protected by their own governments, there were attacks on those who converted to the Protestant expression of Christianity and who were far more vulnerable. Pressure was applied by levying greater taxation on them, by families abandoning them, or even by imprisonment and persecution.

As'ad Shidyaq[16] was one of the first Arabic-speaking people to be converted by the missionaries in Lebanon. He became the first Protestant martyr in the Middle East and has been held up as a prime witness to the persecution of Protestant converts by the ancient churches. As'ad was born in 1798 in Hadet near Beirut. He was skilled in both Arabic and Aramaic, and for a few years he worked both for the Maronite patriarch and the Emir of Mount Lebanon. In 1825 he was engaged to teach Aramaic to the American missionary Jonas King and also to edit King's Arabic sermons. Through this work, As'ad was introduced to the Bible and Protestantism. Initially the reaction of the patriarch was disbelief, but this quickly became a threat of excommunication if As'ad did not sever all connections with the "Bible men." There were many efforts by the patriarch to persuade As'ad to abandon the new teachings. However, As'ad took a position similar to that of Martin Luther at Worms: "If someone were found who could prove that I am in error and that there is no salvation for me save through following the Pope, or at least to demonstrate to me that it is lawful to do so, I am prepared to abandon all my subjective views and submit to anyone in the Lord. But without evidence that they are in error, I cannot forsake them and submit to the obedience of the blind."[17] Such steadfast conviction provoked the Vatican through the Sacred Congregation Propaganda de Fide, which wrote on October 26, 1826, to Patriarch Yusuf Hubaysh:

> Most illustrious and respected Eminence: Tearful news has reached this Holy Congregation about a ruinous development among the students of the college of 'Ayn Waraqa. It is said that the student As'ad Shidyaq has become Protestant and that he is in full collaboration with the chiefs of the English Protestants resident in Beirut, and that not only is he implicated in his own heresy but also that he is determined to deceive others, teaching and debating against the Catholics to the grave scandal of pious people. In addition to anxieties caused by the aforementioned student, it has been reported that other teachers in this school have exhibited suspicious and ruinous behavior. Your Eminence knows how critically important it is for you to build a fence without delay to prevent so great an evil if indeed it is present. You must urgently investigate to find out the truth of these allegations, and then to take whatever remedies your wisdom and piety see fit to stop the development of this encroaching

evil. Inform this Holy Congregation in full detail about this, and about the nature of the advisers and teachers of the college so that this Holy Congregation might devote itself to another course that will result in the spiritual welfare of this nation that has always been characterized by its attachment to our holy religion. With great desire we anxiously await your reply.[18]

Three years later, having refused to abandon his Protestant beliefs, which he held were based on Scripture, As'ad Shidyaq was tortured to death as a prisoner in the monastery of Qannubin. His death was regarded by the leaders of the ancient church as a warning against conversion to Protestantism by any Lebanese person. The persecution of Protestant converts was a policy not only of the Maronite patriarch of Lebanon but also of the Coptic pope of Alexandria, Demetrius II (patriarch 1862–1870) and is documented in Palestine as well. However, intra-Christian converts, excommunicated and persecuted by their mother church, became the nucleus for several Protestant churches that are found today throughout the entire Middle East region.

The occupation of Syria by Ibrahim Pasha and the spread of Protestant missions thereafter triggered a Catholic countermission and pushed Catholic orders to renew their presence in the Middle East, competing for the souls of Orthodox Christians from various denominations. In the context of the Second French Empire under Napoleon III (1852–1870) with its reverse policy and promotion of the Catholic Church, schools, and orders, Catholic missions started to mushroom in the Middle East. The Jesuits were the first to return to the Middle East upon the request of the Greek Catholic patriarch Maximus Mazlum. During the reign of Ibrahim Pasha in Syria, they were able to open their first monasteries and schools in Zahleh (1833), Bikfaya (1833), and Beirut (1839). In response to the establishment of the first Protestant seminary by William Thompson in Abey in 1835, the Jesuits opened a Catholic seminary in Ghazir in 1843, and following the establishment of the Syrian Protestant College (later to become the American University in Beirut), the Jesuits opened St. Joseph University in 1881. The Jesuit expertise in education spread from Lebanon to

Egypt, where they opened a seminary in al-Ma'adi, Cairo in 1879, followed by other educational enterprises in Alexandria (1844) and Cairo (1889). Like their Protestant counterparts, the Jesuits played an important role in the Arab Renaissance, through their Institute of Oriental Studies and their journal *al-Mashreq*.[19]

Like the Protestant missions and in a colonial fashion, the different Catholic missions divided the Middle East among themselves with each order focusing on a specific geographic area. While the Jesuits concentrated their efforts among the Maronites in Lebanon and the Copts in Egypt, the Dominicans were mainly interested in the Syriac and Chaldean Churches in Iraq, especially in Mosul (1840). Besides Iraq, the Dominicans were also interested in Palestine, and in 1884 they were able to renew their presence in Jerusalem, culminating with the inauguration of the École Biblique in 1890.[20] While the Lazarist Fathers and their female branch of the Sisters of Charity were very much engaged in Lebanon, they had monasteries in Turkey and were charged to represent the Holy See in Persia.[21] Another important Catholic order that came to the Middle East in the mid-nineteenth century was the Brethren of Christian Schools, founded by John Baptist de La Salle. Their focus was on education and higher education. They founded their first institutions in Turkey and Egypt (1847), and in Palestine (1878). The Franciscans spread throughout the eastern Mediterranean in Palestine, Lebanon, Syria, Cyprus, and Egypt.

The establishment of the bishopric of the United Church of England and Ireland in Jerusalem in 1841 was another reason for alarm within certain segments of the Roman Catholic Church in the Vatican, Germany, and beyond. In 1842, one year later, the Sacred Congregation Propaganda de Fide began to study the feasibility of nominating a papal delegate to Jerusalem with the title patriarch. However, this idea faced strong opposition from two sides: On the one hand, the Custos, the guardian of the Holy Land, saw this nomination as a threat to his authority and jurisdiction over that area. The French government, which had been named the sole protectorate of Roman Catholic Christians within the empire, also found the idea disquieting.

As a consequence, the concept of the nomination remained in abeyance between 1842 and 1846.

Two major events in 1846 led to the final papal decision to name a patriarch for Jerusalem.[22] The first major event was the arrival in Jerusalem of the Swiss bishop Gobat, appointed by the king of Prussia, who began a new focus on "reforming the oriental churches." Rome saw in this a direct threat since it desired to attract the oriental churches to unite with Rome. The second major event was the election of a new pope in 1846, Pius IX, who was deeply interested in encouraging Eastern Christians to unite with Rome via a policy of establishing Catholic bishoprics throughout the world. During his reign he established twenty-nine archbishoprics and 132 bishoprics. In 1847 Joseph Valerga, a thirty-four-year-old Italian priest, was ordained a bishop and sent to Jerusalem as the first Latin patriarch of Jerusalem. Since there was already a "bishop of Jerusalem," the bishop from the United Church of England and Ireland, it became important for the Roman Catholic Church to use a more elevated title of patriarch and to name him Latin patriarch of Jerusalem. With this new title, the Roman Catholic Church responded to the newly established Anglican episcopate and repositioned itself in the center. These developments forced the Greek Orthodox patriarchate to reestablish residence in Jerusalem in 1845 after having been located for decades in Constantinople. Thus, Jerusalem became the official seat of three patriarchates and several bishops, all heads of church bodies. Just as Bishop Gobat invited several German missions to come to work within his jurisdiction, so Patriarch Valerga invited the Sisters of St. Joseph of the Apparition (1848), the Sisters of Nazareth (1855), and the Sisters of Zion (1856).[23]

The competing Protestant and Catholic missions in the Middle East inevitably triggered a reaction within the Orthodox churches. In a manner similar to the Counter-Reformation, which was the Tridentine response to the Reformation, the impact of the newly arrived Protestantism in the Middle East forced the ancient churches to adopt new patterns of response and modern forms of organization, education, and social work—and, indeed, of biblical teaching. Thus, the Presbyterian mission in Egypt in the

mid-nineteenth century provoked what has come to be known as
the "Coptic Enlightenment." As a part of this development, Coptic
pope Cyril IV (papacy 1854–1861) founded the Great Coptic School
to compete with the Presbyterian school system.

Similarly, Presbyterian understanding of and emphasis on the
presbyter led in 1874 to the development of a movement of laity
within the Coptic Orthodox Church typified by the creation of
the so-called Majlis al-Milli, the first of a kind of Coptic communal or congregational council; *majlis* means "a place of sitting" as,
for example, on a council. In 1881, the Coptic Church established
the Coptic Benevolent Society in an effort not to cede social work
in Egypt exclusively to the Catholic and Protestant churches. "In
short, the arrival of the American missionaries meant that Copts
gained a new choice in how they would live and practice their
Christianity. This element of choice then compelled Coptic leaders
of all sectarian backgrounds to rise to the challenge of maintaining
allegiances in a competitive market of Christian ideas. The result,
in the end, was a rejuvenated and more pluralistic culture of Egyptian Christianity."[24] Not only in Egypt but throughout the Middle East, the arrival of Protestants triggered competition between
Protestants and Roman Catholics as well as between Protestants
and Orthodox, a competition for souls, minds, and allegiances.

The Russian ecclesiastical mission[25] in Palestine represented
another example of Orthodox "counter-reformation." Upon the
recommendation of Porfiri Uspenski (1804–1885), a Russian orientalist, archeologist, theologian, and bishop who represented
the "pan-Slavic" movement, a Russian diplomatic mission was
established in 1847 in Jerusalem to counter the influence of
Roman Catholic and Protestant missions. Uspenski directed this
mission from 1848 to 1854. Interrupted by the Crimean War, the
Russian mission reinvented itself in 1857 with a focus on the education of the Orthodox population of Palestine and Syria. More
than 102 Russian Orthodox schools were established, especially
in towns and villages where there was an Orthodox majority.
Supporting the local Arab Orthodox community in its struggles
with and against the Greek hierarchy was another important feature of the Russian mission.

The Russian influence in Palestine was strengthened by the establishment of the Orthodox Russian Society in 1882, known after 1889 as the Imperial Orthodox Palestine Society. Bringing Russian pilgrims to the Holy Land was one of the main activities of this society. In 1882 around two thousand Russians made pilgrimages to Jerusalem; by 1914 that number had grown to over fifteen thousand, which meant that Russia led all countries in pilgrimages to the Holy Land.

Over the course of the years there has been strenuous debate concerning the role of Christian missions in the context of European colonialism. Christian missionaries in the Middle East were often portrayed as "cultural imperialists" or as "agents of the empire." In actuality, it is not possible to conclude that the European Christian mission to the Middle East was unambiguously a colonialist enterprise, nor is it possible clearly to distinguish between the two. What the two had in common was a desire for the expansion of Western Christian and European influence beyond national or geographic borders. The case can surely be made that both phenomena, "mission" and "colonialism," stem from a common European expansionist culture that felt itself superior and powerful enough to bring others who were at a great distance under their military or religious control. Both groups were convinced that they had (European) "products" to offer and that there were "markets" abroad awaiting fulfillment. Without a doubt there were links between the rise of imperialist domination in the Middle East and the spread of the missionary enterprise.

In general, religious identity was linked to national identity: Protestant missions were mainly British, American, and to some extent German; Catholic missions were mainly French, Austrian, and Italian; while the Orthodox mission was exclusively Russian. This meant that intra-European national rivalries and competition in religious missions were two sides of the same coin. This rivalry and competition planted the seeds for sectarian identities that were not previously known in such a form or intensity. The Christian mission schools became tools to not only educate local Christians but to instill in them an allegiance to the "motherland" of the missionaries and a strong loyalty to a specific religious denomination, often even within the same denomination to a specific country (Russian versus Greek for Orthodox) or even order (like Jesuits versus Dominicans). A culture of sectarianism was thereby enhanced, leading later to a weakening of social cohesion and fragmentation of the social fabric in the Middle East.

3

A MASSACRE ON MOUNT LEBANON

The Ottoman Empire was a multireligious and multiethnic empire. Islam provided the backbone, the glue that kept the empire together, as well as the religious legitimacy that the sultan needed, while the millet system gave non-Muslims their autonomy. This flexible and pragmatic administrative system allowed the diverse population enough space to exercise their individual traditions and customs without interference from the empire. In addition, a decentralized tax collection system operated by local and regional nobilities gave the empire durability and stability. Christians benefited from this stability, and their numbers tripled in size. In fact, the percentage of Christians in the Middle East grew from about 7 percent in the fifteenth century under the Mamluks to over 20 percent under the Ottomans toward the end of the nineteenth century.[1] The persecution of Christians under the Ottomans, if any, was rare and localized.

The rise of Muhammad Ali shook this stable three-century-old system. His promise of full equality for Syrian Christians triggered the Ottomans to adopt a series of major reforms that altered the community-based status quo, known as the millet system, and replaced it with the concept of individual Ottoman citizenship. These reforms were an attempt by the empire to elevate the status of non-Muslims, mainly Christians and Jews, but were perceived as de facto putting an end to Muslim supremacy. The changes frightened the Muslim masses, especially the traditional leadership and nobility, who resisted the changes by every means. In addition, the education offered by missionary schools gave Christians better access to economic prosperity and created a new Christian bourgeoisie that competed with the traditional Muslim nobility. These factors, coupled with the fact that Christians also had the right to appeal to European powers for protection in and against Ottoman courts, led Muslims to feel that they were becoming disadvantaged. The growing fear within the political and economic Muslim establishment led to a series of violent outbursts by Muslims against their Christian neighbors in Aleppo in 1850, Mosul in 1854, Nablus in 1856, and Jeddah in 1858, culminating in 1860 in the massacre of Christians by the Druze on Mount Lebanon.[2]

This massacre on Mount Lebanon provides an excellent case study to analyze and understand the politics of persecution. Mount Lebanon in the early nineteenth century was a religiously mixed region with a considerable Christian population spread across the mountain. Maronite Christians constituted the overwhelming majority on the north of the mountain, but there was also a considerable Maronite presence in the southern Druze-dominated region. While these two religious groups made up the majority of Mount Lebanon's population, other religious communities like the Greek Orthodox, Greek Catholics, and Shiites were also present. Christian and Druze shared a common language, culture, and often a shared space in several mixed villages. Yet, within a feudal social order, religious identity was embedded in a socioeconomic system that cut each community into two social strata:

> Ottoman Lebanese society was shaped less by centuries of sectarian tolerance (or strife) than by a social order that, heuristically speaking, cut Mount Lebanon in two. At the top, an elite community regarded its control over religious and secular knowledge as essential to a hierarchical ordering of society. This community included Lebanese notables and those who chronicled their histories, as well as Ottoman officials and religious leaders. It existed above, exploited, and defined itself against the second community, the *ahali*, or the common Druze and Maronite villagers constituting the bulk of indigenous society.[3]

This social order existed within the framework of the Ottoman Empire. Loyalty to the sultan united Christians and Muslims. The occupation of Mount Lebanon by Muhammad Ali's son, Ibrahim

Pasha, disrupted this well-established social system. While the Druze remained loyal to the sultan and rebelled against Ibrahim's army, the Maronites welcomed the new ruler and were armed to suppress the Druze rebellion. Several of the Druze landlords were exiled to Egypt. This created a first rupture on Mount Lebanon. When Muhammad Ali, and later the Ottoman reforms, asserted equality between Christian and Muslim citizens, the Christian peasants who used to work for the exiled Druze notables interpreted this as an end to the existing feudal social structure. They rebelled against their landlord and sought to exercise freedom from and equality with their landlords.

When Ibrahim Pasha's army was defeated by the Ottomans, with the assistance of the British, and Ottoman rule on Mount Lebanon was reestablished, the exiled Druze nobles who returned to reclaim their former properties faced a rebellious Christian peasant community backed by the Maronite patriarch, who called for the reestablishment of a Maronite emirate. Although under Ottoman rule and loyal to the sultan, a Christian denomination was no longer satisfied with its ecclesiastical autonomy and requested political autonomy for the first time. The religious space granted within the millet system and the old feudal social system were no longer adequate. It was not easy to restore Ottoman sovereignty or return to Ottoman business as usual within this new context. The European powers that had come to aid the Ottomans by pushing back Ibrahim Pasha's army had become part of the new equation and had their own interests to pursue. Their new encounter and interaction with the people of Mount Lebanon resulted in major sociopolitical shifts that led to changes in the self-understanding and positioning of the diverse Lebanese communities:

> Britain, France, and the Ottomans regulated different aspects of the colonial encounter and this opened avenues for the indigenous inhabitants of Mount Lebanon to reinterpret their own history, their own communal self-definition, and ultimately their own rigid social order. Power, of course, was crucial because the encounter was never equal; the flow of transformative ideologies and knowledge headed mostly from Istanbul, Paris and London to Mount Lebanon, where

the consequences of this exchange, sectarianism as both knowledge and a practice, was produced.[4]

This fragile sociopolitical situation led to sectarian clashes in 1841. Triggered by a trivial conflict between two individuals (a Druze and a Christian), the conflict escalated to become a conflict between two religious communities over the control of land and culminated in human casualties on both sides. The new situation and the presence of the European powers "created the space for reworked communal identities to emerge in the public sphere."[5] The Druze and Maronite elites and leaders reconstituted themselves not so much as a social class but as representatives of their religiopolitical communities before the European powers. The Druze Nakad Sheikh appealed to the British on behalf of all the Druze, and the Maronite patriarch to France became the spokesperson of the Maronite community. "Neither Maronite nor Druze leaders sought to break with the Ottoman Empire, but each recognized individual European powers as the protectors of their community and as arbitrators of their political destiny, as players who could influence the course of politics as much as and, in some cases, more than the sultan himself."[6] This represented an opportune moment for the European states to "protect" local communities, thereby justifying their interest and involvement in the Ottoman Empire.

The new political constellation that formed after the violence of 1841 led to a joint European-Ottoman decision in December 1842 to partition Mount Lebanon along religious lines. Under the pretext of unifying geography with demography, Mount Lebanon was cut in half. The northern district was meant to be a homogenous "Christian" area ruled by a Christian district governor, and the southern district was to be a distinctly "Druze" region ruled by a Druze district governor. "The logic of partition demanded the unambiguous classification of the local inhabitants into one or another camp, either Christian or non-Christian. . . . New categories of 'Christian' or 'Druze' rule were created alongside the idea of 'mixed' villages and 'minorities.'"[7] Mount Lebanon was communally reinvented: "A public and political sectarian identity replaced a nonsectarian politics of notability that had been the hallmark of pre-reform society."[8]

The partition of Mount Lebanon along sectarian lines proved to be a grave mistake. Social and religious tensions were rising and erupted in 1858 when a Maronite Christian peasant in the north led a rebellion against a Maronite landlord for seizing his land and property. This was a social rebellion within the Maronite community itself. But once the rebellion reached the mixed villages, it took on a sectarian form of Maronite peasants against their Druze landlords. When the Maronite rebels from the north marched to assist and "liberate" their "coreligionists" in the south, a civil war broke out. The Druze armed themselves and were keen to erase all traces of the Maronites in the mixed districts. In a volatile sectarian climate, geography had to be redefined as belonging to one exclusive religious community, with no place whatsoever for another sect. In such a state of tension, security could be achieved only by eliminating the "other" community from one's geography. Within a few weeks in the summer of 1860, around ten thousand Maronite Christians were massacred on Mount Lebanon, several Christian villages destroyed, churches burned, and monasteries plundered by members of the Druze community. This became the bloodiest event in Mount Lebanon's history. What started as a conflict over social class developed within three decades into a full-fledged civil war along sectarian religious lines. Geography could no longer tolerate more than one demography: either Christian or Druze.

This event provides an excellent case study of the politics of persecution, starting with what to call it. How to name such a "bloody event"? Was it a clear case of Christian persecution? Was it a massacre? Or was it a civil war? The label chosen depends very much on one's own standpoint and is strongly linked to politics.

For the American consul in Beirut, Augustus Johnson, the 1860 event was obviously a massacre of Christians by Druze Muslims. In his letter published in the *New York Times* on June 28, 1860, he wrote:

> You have doubtless heard of the horrible massacres that have just been perpetrated upon the poor Christians of Mount Lebanon by the Druses, aided in some cases by Turkish

soldiers. A few facts may give you an adequate idea of the present state of things in Syria. The American Missionaries have estimated the loss sustained by the Christians at 10,500, and that of the Druses about 1,200. The inhabitants of the Christian towns of Deir il Komr and Hasleeiya were brutally slaughtered in cold blood, after a full surrender had been made. Thirty or forty convents have been plundered and burned, and the monks were put death, some of whom were French. Nearly one hundred villages have been burned, and the crops of the peasantry destroyed! Many churches also, have been burned—among them the American-Mission Chapel at Hasleeiya, and the school-houses at Deir il Komr. The facts are enough to strike the civilized world with horror; but there is yet something to be told. It is believed that not less than sixty thousand Christians are now homeless and starving, and have no other hope for subsistence than the charity of the Christian world! More than 5,000 fugitives have been supported by the consuls, missionaries, merchants and convents of Beirut; but this is only a temporary arrangement. Something must be done for the starving, homeless thousands who are now hiding in caves and other secret places until peace shall be declared. Beirut is no longer a place of safety for Christians. Moslem fanaticism is now fully aroused, and the Turkish Government has found it necessary to station a platoon of soldiers in every consul's house for their protection. Thousands of the Christian refugees, and large numbers of the native residents, have fled the country. Indeed, the land is full of misery and the deepest woe. American missionaries, aided by the guards from the American Consulate, have brought away many poor, besieged and persecuted Christians, whose lives have been thus preserved; and the English vessels of war have picked up about 2,000 fugitives, many wounded women and children, who had escaped to the seacoast—and there is still work for them to do. What can be done in the United States for these famishing widows and orphans? I will say nothing now of vengeance, for the European Powers will no doubt exact justice for this great crime; but humanity calls upon me not only to distribute bread to the crowds around my house, but to present their cause to my countrymen, and to arouse their sympathies in behalf of this persecuted people. The King of Greece has sent a sum of money for their present relief, and efforts are being made elsewhere to collect money for that object. America sent food to Ireland and to Greece, and will not something be done for the Christians of Syria?[9]

For Johnson this was not only a massacre but a matter of persecution of "poor Christians" by "Muslim fanatics." It is a horrific act of barbarism that stands in contrast to the civilized Western world. The consul shows clear sympathy with the "plight of the persecuted Christians," with the besieged and displaced orphans and widows. He sees his role not confined only to humanitarian assistance, but to speak on their behalf, to present their case to his countrymen. This paradigm continues to be one of the most dominant of the Western narrative on the plight of the Christians in the Middle East. In this paradigm we depict an orientalist attitude of a superior and civilized Christian West that gazes at a barbaric "Orient" that is Islamic, irrational, anti-Christian, and stuck in a primitive mindset. The West assumes the role of defender and advocate on behalf of Middle Eastern Christians. The consul is aware that the United States has no political role to play here: that is left to the European powers.

The discourse presented by Consul Johnson was the dominant public account in Europe and was repeated in the French, British, Austrian, Prussian, and Russian press. But this discourse also had a local echo and was popular among Maronite Christians and clergy, who recounted the horror and pleaded for sympathy and protection from their French Catholic allies. There have always been some Middle Eastern Christians who have looked to the West for protection, aid, and political backing. For the French, such a plea was all that was needed to galvanize military intervention, and France immediately deployed six thousand soldiers in Lebanon. The victimization of Christians in the Middle East was an excellent pretext for Western political and military intervention. The Maronite patriarch was thankful for French protection that, he hoped, could lead to Maronite sovereignty and a possible autonomous Christian Lebanese entity.

What was clear cut for the French was more complex for the British. Although the British press expressed sympathy for the plight of the Christians, British realpolitik was inclined to look at the massacred Maronites not as mere helpless victims but as a party in the conflict. The fact that they were Catholics rather than Protestants, and allies of France, weakened British sympathy. On the other hand, Britain felt unable to side wholeheartedly with the Druze despite them being British allies because of the Druze religious affiliation with Islam. The Druze were depicted on the one hand as warlike, hungry tigers and on the other as disciplined and savagely brave. Charles Henry Churchill, the British consul in Syria, described the 1860 event as a civil war without civility. About the events in Baalbek, he wrote:

> The Christians were being hunted down like wild beasts, their houses fired, their men slain, their women violated. . . . Even from the mosques and minarets the shout for blood arose; and, mingled with the muezzin's call to prayer, might be heard a cry informing the faithful that by an imperial firman the Christians were devoted to destruction, and their wives and properties had become a lawful prey.[10]

Describing the events in Deir al-Qamar, he continued:

> The slaughter next commenced. Whenever a Christian was seen, he was shot or cut down. Flames at the same time burst forth in various places. Dark volumes of smoke hung brooding over the town. The shouting, swearing and screaming was appalling. The priests fled to their churches, and were slain at the foot of the altars. All who followed them to the sacred edifices were butchered on the pavement. . . . All the horrors of Hasbeya were now renewed. The blows given by hatchets, axes and billhooks, as they fell on the human body, sounded like those of woodcutters felling a forest. Every kind of blasphemy, imprecation, and insult, which heart could devise or tongue pronounce, was vented by the Druze on their helpless victims. Did any try to conceal themselves, they were hunted out and dragged forth by the Turks. Did a Druze perchance show mercy, the Turk was there to taunt him with his weakness and urge him to complete the deed.[11]

We can clearly see a similar orientalist perspective in Churchill's account. He indulges in painting the scenes of the massacres of defenseless Christians very poignantly. The Druze are depicted as bloodthirsty, savage rapists whose aggression is almost inherent to Islam. Here and there, one finds some sympathy with the Druze who were almost forced by the Ottomans to continue their aggression. Yet in this lengthy account of the 1860 massacres, there is no mention of the context, the fact that the Druze were the allies of Britain, and that it was Britain that had earlier supplied the Druze with arms. The 1860 events took place over several weeks. Churchill retrospectively (1862) shed tears over the Christian fate, but no political action was taken in a timely manner to come to the rescue of those same Christians. This is a recurring Western pattern when talking about persecuted Christians. Too many words of sympathy combined with political apathy and no real effort to change the sociopolitical situation. Empathy for persecuted Christians is one thing, realpolitik and economic interests are another. The situation of Middle Eastern Christians is nothing more than an orientalist cliché that is subordinate to Western interests.

Although Churchill uses the term "civil war" to describe the bloody event, one is nevertheless left with the impression that it was a religious war between the Maronites and the Muslim Druze. The way the "civil war" is described leads one to believe that it was not at all civilized since the images conjured up depict the Druze and the Ottomans as savages, beasts, and warmongers. This stands in clear contrast to the rational, civilized, and thus superior Christian Europe.

Churchill was not the first to use the term "civil war" to describe the 1860 event. The first person to use it was a native Protestant intellectual, Butrus Bustani. His perspective is very interesting and important to look at because it combines the "urgency of proximity"[12] on the one hand and a certain distance on the other. While Bustani was a native of Mount Lebanon and of a Maronite background, he was a Protestant convert who resided in Beirut. Having worked as a dragoman to the British armed forces in 1840, for the American Consulate (1851–1862), and for almost two decades with American missionaries (1841–1859), he had an insider's perspective on Western attitudes and was critical (but not too critical) of the West. Having experienced a kind of religious conversion at the hand of American missionaries, he was eager not to be a mere "Western plant" in the Middle East. This led him to push for the establishment of a "native evangelical church" in 1848, abandoning his work with the American mission in 1859. The second Ottoman reforms introduced in 1856 gave him tremendous hope for a future based on equality between Christians and Muslims under Ottoman law, and rule based on a shared Arabic culture and identity. Work on the story of As'ad Shidyaq, the first Protestant martyr, tortured and killed in a Maronite monastery, published in early 1860, opened Bustani's eyes to the dangers of religious fanaticism. It is this long and rich journey, and hybrid identity, that gave Bustani a unique perspective. The civil war in 1860 pushed him to publish, under the anonymous name of "patriot," a series of eleven "religiopolitical pamphlets" entitled Clarion of Syria, to alert the people of Lebanon to the vicious effects of civil war.[13] The first pamphlet was issued on September 29, 1860, three months after the end of the civil war, and the last in April 1861. His goal in these pamphlets was not to describe the horrors of the civil war as Johnson and Churchill did but to draw lessons from it that might help the people in Mount Lebanon and the Middle East to move forward.

The contrast between Bustani's account and those of Johnson and Churchill is like day and night. Although Bustani is not a politician, he is very aware of the geopolitical context that led to this war: "Syria lies between two countries, Egypt and the Ottoman Empire, which have often pulled it in different directions. Within a single generation, it has tilted at times to one side and at other times to the other. In both instances, Syria has unfortunately found itself in the peripheries of each empire."[14] The invasion of and withdrawal from Syria under Ibrahim Pasha, and the changes to the status quo that occurred, were, as discussed previously, one of the major reasons that led to the violence. Bustani was not blind or naive. He was aware that alongside the external geopolitical aspects, there were internal ills as well. "Syria is also the birthplace and stage of many conflicting civil and religious prejudices whose organization and origins are at odd with each other."[15] However, for him, the problem was not Islam or any other religion but the prejudices that develop between different groups.

> This wicked concept [prejudice] takes different colors at every stage. It once took the form of notable rivalries such as the one between the Qaysi and Yamani factions, and then between the Jumblats and the Yasbakis. One of its ugliest forms has appeared in these last few years. It took on names sacred to its people—names like Christian and Druze, and then Muslim and Christian. These sacred names had long been buried under the previous ones of the Qaysi/Yamani and Jumblat/Yasbak splits, but the concept has appropriated these sacred and old names, realizing the magical and formidable force that they hold when used in the context of what the people of our country call "the source of attachment"—that is, kinship. As such, this wicked concept served the machinations of the most powerful leaders of prejudices with the result that its power multiplied and its effects became far-reaching.[16]

The problem for Bustani was not religion as such or Islam but in the preconceived ideas and stereotypes about the other, irrespective of whether it was the social other or religious other. Prejudices are even found within the same Druze community and represented by the two dominant Druze families: the Jumblats and the Yazbaks. Prejudice is not something inherent in Middle Eastern people and religions but is also widespread in the West against Arabs, Middle Easterners, and Muslims.[17]

The other problem is the instrumentalization of religion for sociopolitical gain by leaders who propagate confessional fanaticism and sacrifice the welfare of the whole community for their own personal interests.[18] The fact that Bustani belonged to a small Protestant community may have enabled him to be critical of the political and religious leaders of Mount Lebanon. His work as a dragoman with the British and American Consulates made him critical of foreign interests as well. "Foreign political intervention may temporarily benefit some individuals, but we strongly believe that it is harmful to all countries. In a country like this one that is home to different races, rife with rooted differences and opposing views regarding foreign intervention, the latter is

especially harmful given the different political and religious interests of the intervening powers."[19] Bustani was the first person to
introduce the term "civil war" for the 1860 events. He provided
a very "modern" analysis of the 1860 civil war as a social conflict
between civilians using arms, within corrupt political structures
and foreign interventions, where prejudice is utilized and religious fanaticism is instrumentalized for personal gain. Although
his pamphlets often appear like Christian sermons with multiple
biblical references, there is no place for a genre of victimology
or Christian persecution. Bustani does not demonize the Druze
either. "What has befallen us, now that we see over there a man
hiding in a cave, and another who has taken shelter in the thick
woods among wild animals, and yet another who, like the brother-
slayer Cain, is a fugitive who has lost his way with no one calling
him in?"[20] Contrary to Johnson and Churchill, who demonized the
Druze as wild beasts, when Bustani talks about wild animals, he
means animals and not people. The Cain paradigm here is care-
fully chosen. Though there is an aggressor and a victim, they are
and remain siblings and compatriots: "You drink the same water,
you breathe the same air. The language you speak is the same, and
so are the ground you tread, your welfare, and your customs. You
may still be intoxicated from drinking your compatriots' blood,
or disoriented by the calamities you have suffered. But very soon
you must wake up from this stupor and realize the meaning of my
advice and where your welfare lies."[21] Bustani introduced here the
concept of patriotism as an antidote to confessional fanaticism,
and thus to sectarianism. To combat sectarianism, it was important to Bustani for there to be a clear separation between civil and
spiritual authorities.[22] Part of the problem for Bustani was that the
religious authorities on Mount Lebanon were assuming a political
role, while "civil" authority was based on belonging to a specific
sect or social status rather than qualification. In such a context,
sectarian identity becomes the driving factor and not the love of
the homeland. It is only within the "Patria," the homeland, that
diverse children can meet on an equal footing, with rights and
responsibilities[23] and under a unifying social contract within the
larger Ottoman political framework.[24]

For Bustani, the homeland was not confined to Mount Lebanon but to Greater Syria, the land between Egypt and Turkey. Within Syria diverse religious, social, and ethnic groups share the same culture: the Arab culture. Thus, he emphasized the importance of the Arabic language, common roots, and a common destiny. Bustani was calling for an Arab awakening as the base for unity in diversity.[25] In Bustani's view, this focus on Arab identity would create a "meta-identity" that would accommodate the multiple ethnic and religious sub-identities, thereby preventing internal fragmentation as well as external exploitation.

Bustani is not calling for a "secular ecumenism" because he writes clearly as a concerned Christian. He is certainly aware that religious identities can be part of the problem, but for him personally, it is crystal clear that faith is part of the solution. It is his faith that led him to love his homeland (*watan*), and it is this faith that leads him to love his "other" neighbor, even his enemy, as himself.[26]

This vision introduced by Bustani in the Clarion of Syria was translated by him into a very concrete program. Two years after publishing those pamphlets, Bustani founded al-Madrasah al-Wataniya, the national school, where in an ecumenical spirit, Christians, Druze, and Muslims could study together. This school must be understood as a critique of the many missionary schools that Bustani came to know and sometimes to teach in: confessional schools that aimed to proselytize their pupils to a certain sect. Bustani's school started with 115 students and emphasized religious freedom and equality. Pupils were to be accepted "from all sects, millets, and races without discriminating against their personal beliefs or any attempt at proselytizing and (should be given) full license to carry out their religious duties."[27] Although pupils should learn different languages and be globally aware, the main language of instruction was Arabic. Bustani was aware that sectarian schools led to the fragmentation of society and potential tensions. The need was, therefore, for a national school that would educate future generations in Syria to love their country, their neighbor, and to cherish their faith and their Arabic culture.

The civil war was interpreted in two totally different ways. For Western European politicians, Western missionaries, and the Maronite clergy, it was clearly a massacre and an act of Christian persecution. They saw the Ottoman Empire as a Muslim state with oppressed Christian "minorities" that needed to be liberated and protected. For Bustani, it was a civil war with arms where sectarian identities were instrumentalized locally and exploited internationally. Bustani did not want to put himself in the shoes of a Christian victim but used his faith to assume responsibility for casting a new vision for Greater Syria.

4

AGENTS OF RENAISSANCE

European penetration into the Middle East through education, trade, and political treaties brought major socioeconomic changes to the Ottoman Empire. In return for pushing Ibrahim Pasha out of Greater Syria, the Ottomans had to make major economic concessions to Britain in 1838. These included the abolition of all monopolies and trade restrictions and opening Egypt and Syria to the British, and later to all European merchants. Europe started to look at the Middle East as an important source of raw materials as well as a new outlet for European markets. Europe was seen as the center of gravity that encompassed political power, knowledge, religion, and economic activity. It was in this context that the term Middle East was coined to distinguish it from the Far East. The economy of the Middle East region had to be included in and to serve European economic interests. This had a major impact on the development of several key cities in the Ottoman Empire.

In order to grow enough silk to satisfy French markets, many Lebanese peasants left their mountain village homes and relocated in coastal areas. Beirut became one of the leading ports in the Middle East, its population growing from a few thousand at the beginning of the nineteenth century to over one hundred thousand toward the end.[1] Alexandria became a center for the cotton industry and attracted many people from Upper Egypt; its population exploded from a few thousand at the beginning of the century to nearly a quarter of a million toward the end.[2] The Jaffa orange, known as the *shamouti*, emerged in the nineteenth-century Ottoman Empire as an important, superior-quality fruit. Its thick skin made it easy to export over days in sailing vessels, not only along the Mediterranean coast but as far as England and Germany. The orange industry was an important factor in the development of Jaffa from a city of three thousand inhabitants at the beginning of the nineteenth century to a major economic center and regional port of forty thousand people with a very affluent Christian community prior to the First World War.[3] A Christian commercial middle class emerged in each of these port cities and along the Mediterranean coast.

This socioeconomic shift from rural to urban became increasingly visible as large numbers of Christians left their traditional agricultural occupations to become merchants and businesspeople. Language skills acquired at Christian schools gave these people a competitive edge over their Muslim neighbors. Contacts with European business communities provided new venues for the export of agricultural products and import of manufactured goods. Palestinian Christian merchants from Bethlehem exhibited their olive wood and mother-of-pearl products at the Philadelphia Centennial Exposition in 1876, the World's Columbian Exposition in Chicago in 1893, and the Louisiana Purchase Exposition in St. Louis in 1904.[4] Transformation of the agrarian sphere and the expansion of trade with Europe led to the monetization of the economy. Money became the universal medium of exchange, leading by the 1840s to the opening of commercial banks in the Ottoman Empire. Commercial European banks were followed by government banks and by smaller private banks. Many of these private banks were owned by Greek and Armenian Christians as well as by Jews.

Education at the mission schools and the language skills acquired, plus the mobility from village to town that took place in the second half of the nineteenth century, paved the way for Christian emigration toward the end of the century. Of the 86,111 Syrians who emigrated to the United States between 1899 and 1914, 90 percent were estimated to be Christian.[5] The same is true of the 330,000 Lebanese who emigrated between 1860 and 1914. "Among those who had emigrated by 1932, 123,397 were Maronites, 57,031 were Greek Orthodox, and 26,627 were Melkites (Greek Catholics) but only 36,865 were Muslims and Druzes."[6] Of the Syrian immigrants arriving in the United States between 1899 and 1910, 46.7 percent were literate, many of them graduates of Protestant schools. By 1914 approximately half of the Christian community of Bethlehem and a third of the neighboring city of Beit Jala had emigrated to Latin America. Today, Latin America has the largest Palestinian diaspora outside the Arab world, with an estimated half a million Palestinians and the largest "Palestinian" Christian population. The largest number of "Latin Americans with Palestinian roots"[7] reside in Chile, while the highest percentage is in Honduras (3 percent). Most of the first immigrants to the New World worked as merchants, many becoming extremely successful. Several Arab and Christian immigrants who were authors became active in the diaspora and formed an Arab-American literary society known as the Pen League. Its aim was to revive the Arabic language and modernize it from its ancient style. These authors included Nasib Arida, Abdul Massih Haddad, Jibran Khalil Gibran, Amin Rihany, Elia Abu Madi, and Mickail Naimy.

The introduction of the printing press[8] was fundamental to the modernization of the Middle East, paving the way for the democratization of education, the spread of religious and nationalistic ideas, and a literary renaissance. The printing press was known in the Middle East as early as the late sixteenth century, but they were found almost exclusively in monasteries in Lebanon and used only for the printing of liturgical and religious texts. In 1798 Napoleon brought a printing press to Egypt that he used initially for his troops and then for the scientific delegation that accompanied him. Later, Muhammad Ali utilized it for his project of literary and scientific revival. A decade later, another printing enterprise was established in Malta by the London Missionary Society; it was intended for use in the society's missionary endeavors. This printing press was moved to Beirut in 1831 and put under the auspices of the American missionaries there. This triggered the Jesuits to inaugurate the Imprimerie Catholique in 1844. These latter two printing presses played an important role in the Arab Renaissance, and their fonts became a trademark known as the "American Script" versus the "Jesuit Script." Several of the employees who were trained in these two printing presses went on to establish their own private presses in the second half of the nineteenth century. By the mid-nineteenth century there were four publishing houses in Jerusalem: the Franciscans (1846), British Protestants (1848), Armenians (1848), and Greek Orthodox (1852). Later, three additional Protestant publishing houses were established in the Middle East, the most famous operated by the Syrian Orphanage at the Schneller School in Jerusalem, then later in Khirbet Kanafar, Lebanon. Additionally, it should be noted that Pope Cyril IV of Alexandria introduced the Egyptian Coptic Church to the printing and publication of religious and educational texts, and that the Dominican Press in Mosul, Iraq, came to be of considerable importance.

The influx of printing presses led to the publication of newspapers. The first newspaper to be published by Arabs for Arabs appeared in 1816 in Iraq. A few years later, Mohammad Ali, in his zeal to establish a modern state, opened the first Arabic publishing house in Egypt, where two newspapers were printed. While most newspapers in the first half of the nineteenth century were owned by governments or religious institutions, during the second half of the century an increasing number of individuals, Christians among them, operated such newspapers. In 1858, Khalil al-Khoury established the first newspaper in Beirut with the name *Hadiqqat al-Achbar*. In 1875 the *al-Ahram* newspaper was established in Alexandria by two Lebanese Greek Catholic (Melkite) brothers, Bishara and Saleem Takla. Significantly, Saleem Takla began his studies with the Protestant missionary Cornelius Van Dyke and continued at the national school in Abey founded by Butrus al-Bustani. In addition to their involvement with the development of newspapers, Christians participated in the launching of significant magazines and journals. Yacoub Sarrouf, another student of both Van Dyck and Bustani, started a new "scientific" magazine called *al-Muqtataf*, and in 1892 Jurji Zeidan, a graduate of the Protestant College, started the magazine *al-Hilal*. The influence of the American missionaries and the Protestant movement is clearly visible in these journalistic developments. The zeal of the Protestant missionaries to spread the gospel no doubt influenced the zeal of the Arab Christian publishing pioneers for the spread of knowledge, science, and enlightenment. By the time of World War I, publishing was no longer an exclusively Christian endeavor but was widespread. There were 283 newspapers and journals in Egypt alone and 34 in Palestine.

Education proved to be one of the most important keys to the socioeconomic transformation of the Middle East region in general and of the Christian communities of the region in particular. At the beginning of the nineteenth century, only pure religious schools—Muslim schools known as Katatib and Christian schools associated with Orthodox, Maronite, or Franciscan monasteries—existed in the Ottoman Empire. European and American missionaries, and Roman Catholic religious orders, brought new theories and practices of education. Their schools retained religion as their base but added disciplines such as the natural sciences, mathematics, history, and geography. The language of the sponsoring agency was also taught—English, German, French, Italian, Russian, or Greek. Between these groups—especially Protestants, Roman Catholics, and (Russian) Orthodox—there was a fierce competition for the minds and souls of the people of the Middle East. Even as the very existence of "religious" schools was called into question in nineteenth century Europe, the majority of schools created in the Middle East during that century were Christian. It seemed as though church bodies that could not open religious schools in their home countries concentrated on new schools in their mission fields. By 1870 the Jesuits had established more than 500 schools in the Middle East, and by 1904 there were 3,397 Roman Catholic missionaries in that part of the world, two-thirds of them French.[9] By 1912 there were 12,800 students enrolled in British Protestant schools, 34,317 in American Protestant schools, 59,414 in French Catholic schools, and between 10,000 and 15,000 in Russian Orthodox schools. This compared to a total of 81,226 students in governmental schools.[10] By 1917 in Palestine alone there were 116 Roman Catholic, 100 Russian Orthodox, 52 Protestant, and 22 Greek Orthodox schools. This total of 290 schools compared to 174 schools operated by the government. Anglican schools were found mainly in rural areas,

German and French schools in urban centers, while the Russian Orthodox schools were located primarily in Orthodox villages.

Alongside the "normal" schools, Christian missionaries introduced vocational training schools that taught handicrafts or professions. An excellent example of such a school was the Syrian Orphanage,[11] founded in Jerusalem in 1860 by the German Protestant missionary Johann Ludwig Schneller (1820–1896). Schneller was not interested in raising "pious talkative Christians." He wanted to train Christians to be capable of sustaining themselves and their families with a profession. He introduced vocational education in the new professions that were emerging in the changed socioeconomic climate of the times: bookbinders, tailors, shoemakers, ceramicists, cooks, bakers, and mechanics. Schneller's school and similar ones created by the Roman Catholic Salesian Order thus introduced a new social class of skilled craftspeople into the Middle East.

Originally established for cultivating new Christian followers and converts, the mission schools became important elements in the renaissance of the Arab world. "Throughout much of the nineteenth century, there had been tension, particularly in the Protestant missionary enterprise, between evangelical efforts to convert Muslims, Jews, and Eastern Christians to Protestantism and the view of modernization—of ideas and lifestyle—that must precede true conversion. This has been referred to as the 'Christ-culture dialectic,' and it underlay the conflict between a focus on evangelistic preaching and conversion on the one hand, and on education and economic development on the other."[12]

The closure of the American Protestant Theological Seminary in Abeih, Lebanon, in 1878 became a turning point in the history of American missions in the Middle East. The American missionaries were gradually becoming aware of the fact that the need in the region was not so much for hundreds of pastors and preachers but for medical doctors, pharmacists, economists, and other professionals. The failure of the American missionaries in their efforts at proselytism led them to reinvent themselves as agents of secular and liberal higher education. The failure of their efforts to "Christianize" the region led the missionaries to shift their efforts in the direction of "civilizing," the preparation of students for secular and utilitarian employment.[13] Following in the Protestant footsteps, the Jesuits saw themselves forced to open their own institution of higher education, known as the Jesuit University of Beirut, in 1881. This started by offering degrees in philosophy and theology then expanding a few years later to medicine and pharmacy.

From an early stage, female education was an integral part of educational missions. As early as 1825 the first school for girls was started by the American mission in Beirut and led the way in 1834 to the establishment, by the wife of the pioneer missionary Eli Smith, of the first regular girl's school in Syria. In a famous speech of 1848 entitled "A Lecture on the Education of Women,"[14] Butrus al-Bustani highlighted the importance of education to enable women to manage households and care for their children. Renegotiating the role of women, Bustani extended a woman from being the guardian of her home to becoming guardian of the homeland, and thus an important player in the process of civilization and in building a modern Syrian-Arab society. Hundreds of girls' schools were started in the second half of the nineteenth century throughout the Ottoman Empire, most of them by the French, English, American, and German missions. Female education was seen as a necessity by the growing middle class to whom it was increasingly clear that educated and caring motherhood was essential to the progressive modernization of the Middle Eastern nations. By the end of the nineteenth century, especially for middle-class intellectuals, education alone for women was not seen as sufficient. The liberation of women and the creation of a "new woman" became the task to pursue.[15]

From the time of Napolean's invasion of Egypt in 1798 to the beginning of the First World War, the Middle East experienced a rapid transformation, largely due to the educational work of Christian missions. It is estimated that over 50 percent of the Middle East region's student body were educated in Christian schools. It is not an exaggeration to claim that Christian schools shaped the entire Middle East. Their graduates often pursued advanced studies at the leading universities of America and Europe. They were found everywhere in positions of influence and importance.

Once educated and empowered, Middle Eastern Christians started to feel the colonial aspects of European Christian missions and agencies. They were not satisfied with being mere objects of the mission and under the thumb of European "masters." A desire emerged among many Christian communities to gain greater independence from the foreign mission agencies. It is revealing to study the responsiveness of those agencies to the general quest for greater independence. American missionaries, who at that time did not represent an empire, were the most sympathetic to that quest. "In 1870, the American Presbyterians decided that the Egyptian Evangelical Church had grown sufficiently to warrant greater autonomy in a system of Arabic-speaking congregations joined in a presbytery. They therefore decided to separate the American mission formally from the Egyptian Evangelical Church and to cede presbyterial control to the latter. In good American fashion, they wrote a constitution to establish these principles of church government."[16] In 1878 this led Khedive Tawfiq, viceroy of Egypt, to officially recognize the Protestant community in Egypt as a distinct Christian *taifa* (sect). Developments in other parts of the Middle East took longer. It was not until 1920 that the National Evangelical Synod of Syria and Lebanon was able to gain independence from the American mission.

Similar developments took place within the Anglican churches established by the Church Mission Society (CMS). By 1871–1872 the importance of creating a local synod for the Anglican congregations in Palestine was felt. The negotiations between the CMS and the local pastors were difficult, however, and a native synod did not come into being for twenty-four years. The CMS was not prepared to grant independence either to the indigenous clergy or to their schools. Finally, in 1905, the Regulations of the Palestinian Native Church Council were adopted, and an Anglican Synod was established with its base in Jerusalem.

Similar developments took place within the Greek Orthodox Christian community. Although these churches had a lengthy history in the Middle East, during the early Ottoman period they came under heavy Greek influence. Their patriarch became a Greek national. A movement began in the late nineteenth century within the Orthodox churches of Greater Syria for the "Arabization" of both the liturgy and the hierarchy. In Palestine the Arabization of the Greek Orthodox Church was supported by the Russian Orthodox mission. Porfiri Uspenski, the founder of the Russian ecclesiastical mission, sparked ethnic consciousness among Orthodox Arabs based on an Arab nationalism that sought independence from the Greek hierarchy.[17] Efforts to Arabize the Orthodox churches began as early as 1872 and reached their zenith between 1899 and 1908. However, all these attempts failed. The absence of Russian support after 1917 and the revolution in the homeland weakened the Arab Orthodox community and left the hierarchy under Greek control, where it still remains. In contrast, in Syria and Lebanon the patriarchate became authentically Arab toward the end of the nineteenth century.

European penetration into the Middle East brought not only modernization, education, and renaissance, but also Zionism, nationalism, and ultimately, colonialism. These three elements of the nineteenth-century European encounter with the Middle East were seeds for future conflicts in the region.

5

CHRISTIAN ZIONISM

Jews have been part and parcel of the fabric of the Middle East and North Africa. Within the multireligious and multiethnic nineteenth-century Ottoman Empire, Jews made up over 1 percent of the population. Mainly an urban community, they had a strong presence in all major centers, with the largest numbers in Baghdad, Cairo, and Alexandria, followed by Aleppo, Damascus, Beirut, and Jerusalem. There were two other relatively small Jewish centers in Tiberias and Safed.[1] Like Christianity, Judaism was a recognized millet and an integral part of the socioeconomic web of the empire, but without any political claims. It was Anglo-Saxon Christians and British politicians who encouraged the Jews in Europe to think of their religious identity as a basis for a political claim over Palestine.

The Anglo-Saxon world had been obsessed with Jews and Judaism since the time of the Reformation. The interpretation of Judeo-centric prophecy developed over several centuries to become an important theme in British intellectual discourse.[2] At the heart of this interest was a desire to assimilate European Jews fully into Anglo-Saxon culture by converting them to Christianity. Toward this goal, the London Jews Society was established in the early nineteenth century by politically prominent and wealthy evangelical Anglicans. In an age of sectarianism, it did not take much for this religious zeal to develop into a political program within the British colonial framework. If France had adopted a Christian denomination, the Maronites, as their protégés in Lebanon, Britain adopted European Jews as their subcontractors to colonize Palestine.

The occupation of Palestine in 1831 by Ibrahim Pasha, Muhammad Ali's son, triggered this development. The policy of tolerance
by Muhammad Ali toward Christians and Jews enabled John Nicolayson, a missionary of the London Jews Society, to settle in Jerusalem in 1833 and to buy two pieces of land in 1838 with the aim
of building an Anglican church for converted Jews. This coincided
with the opening of a British consulate in Jerusalem. Anthony
Ashley-Cooper, seventh Earl of Shaftesbury,[3] a prominent figure in
the evangelical Anglican movement and a member of the British
House of Commons, followed these developments in Jerusalem
closely. In January 1839 he published an article in the *Quarterly
Review* calling for the settlement of Jews in Palestine.

> The soil and climate of Palestine are singularly adapted to
> the growth of produce required for the exigencies of Great
> Britain; the finest cotton may be obtained in almost unlim-
> ited abundance; silk and madder are the staple of the coun-
> try, and olive oil is now, as it ever was, the very fatness of the
> land. Capital and skill are alone required: the presence of a
> British officer, and the increased security of property which
> his presence will confer, may invite them from these islands
> to the cultivation of Palestine; and the Jews, who will betake
> themselves to agriculture in no other land, having found,
> in the English consul, a mediator between their people and
> the Pacha, will probably return in yet greater numbers, and
> become once more the husbandmen of Judaea and Galilee.[4]

Lord Shaftesbury saw Palestine as a land with great agricultural potential that could serve the economic expansion of the
British Empire and requiring simply the capital and skills that
British Jews possessed to unlock this potential. Political developments in Palestine were accelerating. In 1840 Britain and Austria
decided to aid the Ottomans against Ibrahim Pasha and were
successful in pushing Pasha back from Syria and Palestine, leaving Egypt under his control. While Prussia wanted Palestine to
be under a Christian protectorate, British diplomats were busy
convincing European Jews to claim Palestine politically for themselves under British imperial rule. Less than four months after the
defeat of Ibrahim Pasha's troops in Palestine (on June 14, 1841),
Charles Henry Churchill, the British consulate in Ottoman Syria

who wrote about the civil war on Mount Lebanon, wrote a letter to Sir Moses Montefiore, the president of the Board of Deputies of British Jews, proposing a strategy for a Jewish national claim to Palestine. This letter is very interesting as it shows that it was not the Jews themselves who thought of Palestine as a homeland but Anglo-Saxon evangelical Christians with political clout. In this letter, we read:

> I cannot conceal from you my most anxious desire to see your countrymen endeavour once more to resume their existence as a people.
>
> I consider the object to be perfectly attainable. But, two things are indispensably necessary. Firstly, that the Jews will themselves take up the matter universally and unanimously. Secondly, that the European Powers will aid them in their views. It is for the Jews to make a commencement. Let the principal persons of their community place themselves at the head of the movement. Let them meet, concert and petition. In fact, the agitation must be simultaneous throughout Europe. There is no Government which can possibly take offence at such public meetings. The result would be that you would conjure up a new element in Eastern diplomacy—an element which under such auspices as those of the wealthy and influential members of the Jewish community could not fail not only of attracting great attention and of exciting extraordinary interest, but also of producing great events.
>
> Were the resources which you all possess steadily directed towards the regeneration of Syria and Palestine, there cannot be a doubt but that, under the blessing of the Most High, those countries would amply repay the undertaking, and that you would end by obtaining the sovereignty of at least Palestine. Syria and Palestine, in a word, must be taken under European protection and governed in the sense and according to the spirit of European administration.
>
> It must ultimately come to this. What a great advantage it would be, nay, how indispensably necessary, when at length the Eastern Question comes to be argued and debated with this new ray of light thrown around it, for the Jews to be ready and prepared to say: "Behold us here all waiting, burning to return to that land which you seek to remould and

regenerate. Already we feel ourselves a people. The senti-
ment has gone forth amongst us and has been agitated and
has become to us a second nature; that Palestine demands
back again her sons. We only ask a summons from these
Powers on whose counsels the fate of the East depends to
enter upon the glorious task of rescuing our beloved country from the withering influence of centuries of desolation
and of crowning her plains and valleys and mountain-tops
once more, with all the beauty and freshness and abundance
of her pristine greatness."[5]

Churchill wrote first to Montefiore in Britain in the belief that he
and other influential European Jews should work on lobbying the
five great European powers. Simultaneously, he prepared a petition
to be signed by Ottoman Jews in Syria out of his conviction that
only Ottoman Jews could petition the Porte to "regain a footing in
Palestine" in a kind of autonomy within the Ottoman Empire, yet
under British protection. Churchill was convinced that the latest
developments in Palestine and the restoration of Ottoman sovereignty over Palestine offered an opportune moment to implement such a plan. He wrote: "Political events seem to warrant the
conclusion that the hour is nigh at hand when the Jewish people
may justly and with every reasonable prospect of success put their
hands to the glorious work of National Regeneration."[6]

    It is interesting how Churchill then ends his letter. He is
unsure how Sir Montefiore will interpret his intentions. To ask
British and European Jews to reclaim and settle in Palestine may
have been interpreted in the nineteenth century as wanting to
resolve the "Jewish question" by relocating European Jews to Palestine. Nineteenth-century Europe was eager for the Jewish community to fully assimilate and blend within national settings, with
conversion to Christianity as the best proof of assimilation. Yet,
Jews were projected as an ancient ethnoreligious tribe belonging
to the Middle East that had ended up in Europe by a kind of a
mistake and thus needed to be relocated.[7] Such an idea could be
interpreted as racism. Churchill was, therefore, keen to clarify his
motives, especially as he was unsure whether his idea would appeal
to a British Jewish banker and philanthropist like Montefiore.

He wrote: "If you think otherwise I shall bend at once to your decision, only begging you to appreciate my motive, which is simply an ardent desire for the welfare and prosperity of a people to whom we all owe our possession of those blessed truths which direct our minds with unerring faith to the enjoyment of another and better world."[8] Churchill is assuring Montefiore that his intentions are well intentioned and biblical. For Churchill, the plan was not driven by political calculations but by religious conviction and belief. Thus, Churchill is describing himself as an evangelical Christian Zionist. Christian Zionism[9] preceded Jewish Zionism by half a century. The seed that Churchill planted bore fruit. In 1860 Sir Moses Montefiore sponsored the establishment of the first Jewish colony in Palestine, just outside the Old City in Jerusalem and opposite Jaffa Gate.

Throughout history, Christian Zionists interpreted almost every major political event in the Middle East through the lens of biblical prophecy. Churchill read the defeat of Ibrahim Pasha through this lens. A decade later, the seventh Earl of Shaftesbury read the Crimean War (1853–1856) through this same lens. The immediate cause of the war was a struggle between France and Russia over Christian rights at holy sites, specifically at the Church of the Nativity in Bethlehem. France sided with the Catholics while Russia took the side of the Greek Orthodox monks. Britain decided to aid the Ottomans in their battle against Russia. In this context in 1854 and as an evangelical Christian, the seventh Earl of Shaftesbury was less interested in the holy sites and their control. His interest was who would obtain the rights over the Holy Land: Palestine and Syria. He wrote in his diary:

> The Turkish Empire is in rapid decay; every nation is restless; all hearts expect some great things. . . . No one can say that we are anticipating prophecy; the requirements of it [prophecy] seem nearly fulfilled; Syria "is wasted without an inhabitant"; these vast and fertile regions will soon be without a ruler, without a known and acknowledged power to claim domination. The territory must be assigned to someone or other; can it be given to any European potentate? To any American colony? To any Asiatic sovereign or tribe? Are these aspirants from Africa to fasten a demand on the soil

from Hamath to the river of Egypt? No, no, no! There is a country without a nation; a nation without a country. His own once loved, nay, still loved people, the sons of Abraham, of Isaac, and of Jacob.[10]

As the European empires tussled over resources, trade routes, and the very future of the Ottoman Empire, Lord Shaftesbury saw an opportunity for Britain to "claim domination" over Palestine, and he used British Jews to that end. Shaftesbury's statement blended the biblical language of prophecy with the imperial interests of the British Empire. It was as if Britain was to be the instrument for the fulfillment of these biblical prophecies that had been waiting for generations. God's promises and imperial interests went hand in hand. Evangelical Christians, following Lord Shaftesbury, initially concentrated on the "restoration" to the Jewish people of what was regarded as their ancient homeland, Palestine. This policy may have had less to do with love for the Jews than with anti-Semitism; sending British Jews to Palestine not only served British imperial interests but could, in the unspoken hope of British politicians, solve the Jewish issue. British politicians were uneasy about the political and economic influence of British Jewry inside Britain and were frightened by waves of impoverished Eastern European Jewish migrants flooding into Britain. Alongside the Aliens Act of 1905, Jews could be prevented from coming to Britain by diverting them to their "homeland" of Palestine. With shrinking space for Jews in Europe, the Zionist movement gradually adopted this particular Christian view of history and its use of biblical prophecy to escape Europe, thereby translating Zionism into a real political agenda. In *Der Juden Staat* published in 1896, Theodor Herzl adopted this Anglo-European plan for a Jewish nation-state as an outpost of Western civilization, where British Jews could be the managers with Eastern European Jews as the cheap labor to develop the barren land of Palestine.[11]

The outcome of the First World War gave the movement the breakthrough it was working toward. On November 2, 1917, the first Lord Arthur James Balfour, British foreign secretary, wrote to his colleague in Parliament and prominent British Jewish banker, Baron Walter Rothschild (1868–1937):

> I have much pleasure in conveying to you, on behalf of
> His Majesty's Government, the following declaration of
> sympathy with Jewish Zionist aspirations which has been
> submitted to, and approved by, the Cabinet: His Majesty's
> Government view with favour the establishment in Pales-
> tine of a national home for the Jewish people, and will use
> their best endeavours to facilitate the achievement of this
> objective, it being clearly understood that nothing shall be
> done which may prejudice the civil and religious rights of
> existing non-Jewish communities in Palestine, or the rights
> and political status enjoyed by Jews in any other country.[12]

The timing of this English cabinet decision was not by chance.
The British army, stationed in Egypt, was ready to storm southern Palestine. On November 22, just a few weeks after this declaration, Jerusalem was occupied by the Commander in Chief
of the Egyptian Expeditionary Force Sir Edmund Allenby. The
four-century-long Ottoman occupation of the Middle East came
to an end.

The "biblical promise" now became the imperial promise of
Palestine to the European Jews. This British promise was promoted from Britain's new imperialist agenda of "colonial development." Palestine was thus seen as an important piece in the
emerging puzzle of Britain's future role in the region, particularly
because of its prime coastal location: "There is no doubt whatever
that the agricultural productivity of the country [Palestine] can be
vastly increased; and it is equally certain that with proper harbours
and railways it can become as of old a great highway of communi-
cation between the Mediterranean and the East."[13] Jewish capital
and agricultural know-how would serve this noble imperial project. The "great highway" promised in Isaiah 40 was projected into
the British interest in controlling and protecting trade routes. The
"wasted land" was no longer wasted if tended by European Jews
serving British interests. The land was depicted as "a land without
a people" because the native inhabitants, Christian and Muslims
who made up 95 percent of the population, were portrayed neg-
atively as "non-Jewish communities" who might have "civil and
religious rights" but no national rights since they were not a "people" in the authentic sense of the word. Christian Zionist discourse

openly "constructed friends (Jews) as well as enemies (Muslims and Roman Catholics), while cultivating an occidentocentric discourse that discounted Eastern Christians. These constructions are manifested in contemporary Western discourse surrounding the Israeli-Palestinian conflict that cast Jews within eschatological dramas while demonizing Muslims and casting aspersions on Christians who are Palestinian or sympathetic to the Palestinian national cause."[14]

This sectarian Christian Zionist approach proved to be disastrous in Palestine. The myopic interpretation of biblical prophecy led to the establishment of a political entity in Palestine based on religious affiliation. It gave exclusive national rights to a religious minority, thus discriminating against the followers of the other two religions, Muslims and Christians, who constituted 95 percent of the population of Palestine. It created in Palestine an exclusive sectarian political entity as part of an imperial colonial project implemented by the Zionist movement, with catastrophic implications for the whole region.

6

THE ROAD TO GENOCIDE

In the nineteenth century, the Middle East was characterized by two contradictory yet interdependent movements: colonialism and nationalism. Napoleon's invasion of the Middle East at the turn of the eighteenth to nineteenth century marked the beginning of a new era of European colonialism in the region. First, the European powers moved to colonize the countries close to the Ottoman borders. The French were interested in North Africa. The first colony to fall under French rule was Algeria in 1830. By 1852 the French, after violent conquest, possessed settlements and colonies there. In 1881 France moved closer to the Ottoman Empire by making Tunisia a French Protectorate, France's second colony in North Africa. The French triggered a vigorous competition between European powers for hegemony over North Africa. In 1882 Egypt became a British colony, followed by Sudan in 1889. Libya became an Italian colony in 1911, and the following year, Morocco became a French Protectorate. By the end of World War I, the entire Middle East and North Africa were fully under European control.

While France and Britain were interested in colonizing the Middle East and North Africa, Russia's eyes were on Greece and the Balkans. Greece shared a religious affiliation with Russia since both countries were Orthodox Christian. The Balkan countries, on the other hand, were like the Russian Slavs in terms of ethnicity. In 1832 the Greeks, with assistance from Russia, Britain, and France, were able to break away from the Ottoman Empire and form an independent monarchy. The Greek success triggered similar attempts in many of the European provinces under Ottoman rule. In the late 1870s and in the context of the Russo-Ottoman

War, Romania, Serbia and Bulgaria, all "Orthodox" countries, declared their independence from the Ottoman Empire.

While the colonization of the Middle East and North Africa took place mainly in Muslim countries, the countries that won their independence from the Ottomans were primarily countries with an Orthodox Christian background. Religious identity combined with ethnicity to form the two key ingredients for nationalism and the quest for independence.[1] While the concepts of the Islamic umma and the Muslim caliph dominated in Muslim countries, the notion of the nation-state against a Turko-Islamic empire grew in popularity in Europe in predominantly Christian countries like Greece and the Balkan states.

The Middle East was not totally isolated from the influence of nationalism. Muhammad Ali was the first ruler to dream of challenging a three-hundred-year-old status quo by calling for the formation of a proto-nation-state between the Nile and the Euphrates. The idea of an Arab awakening spread through Christian schools and had a significant impact on both Christians and Muslims in the Middle East as Arab intellectuals who envisioned independence from the Ottomans grew in number. In 1905, Negib Azoury, a Syrian Christian married to a Palestinian Christian, published *The Awakening of the Arab Nation*,[2] in which he called for the establishment of an Arab nation, for the end of Ottoman rule, and for the unification of all churches in Greater Syria as one Catholic Church in which worship would be in the Arabic language. Azoury also expressed opposition to the Zionist movement in this book.

In 1916 the United Kingdom and France, with the assent of Russia, signed a treaty that was initially secret. Known as the Sykes-Picot Agreement, it basically divided the Middle East up between themselves: Syria was occupied by France; Iraq by England; Lebanon came under a French mandate; and Jordan and Palestine under British mandates. Arabs and other inhabitants of the Middle East who had fought in the late nineteenth and early twentieth centuries for liberation from the Ottoman Empire found themselves instead under the control of two European powers. Clearly, the earlier guarantee by the British that the Arabs would have a state of their own stretching from the eastern shore of the Mediterranean to Mesopotamia was not honored.

The Ottoman Empire in the late nineteenth century was marked by European colonialism on the one hand and a rising sense for national identity on the other. Both movements were interwoven: Ideas of nationalism were spread by European schools, and the quest for a nation-state was supported by European powers as a way to weaken the Ottomans. Simultaneously, European colonialism triggered anticolonial sentiments among Muslims and the Christian intelligentsia. It was in this context that Sultan Abdul Hamid II ascended to the throne in 1876. The sultan was eager to continue with the modernization and reform process that had begun a few decades earlier in the belief that this would strengthen the empire against external threats from the European colonial powers, and that reforms and equality between all citizens would consolidate the multireligious and multiethnic fabric of the empire internally. Yet, within the first year of the sultan's reign, Russia declared war on the Ottoman Empire, ending in victory for the Russians. The 1878 Treaty of San Stefano gave independence to Romania, Serbia, Montenegro, and Bulgaria, with the result that the Ottomans lost a huge territory in the north. In the east, the treaty ceded a large area of Georgian and Armenian territories to Russia. The new sultan saw how the European powers were snapping at the Ottoman territory from the left and right. The threat of European interference, and the rising nationalism and quest for independence among the diverse ethnicities within the empire, became a nightmare for the sultan.[3]

The San Stefano Treaty appeared to give hope to other ethnic groups to strive for independence and support from European powers. In 1887 the first Armenian nationalist party, the Social Democrat Hunchakian Party, or Hnchags, was established in Geneva by seven Russian Armenian Marxist students. Three years later the Armenian Revolutionary Federation was founded. Both parties had their roots in East Armenia that had been ceded to Russia, both had socialist roots, and both were a feature of the Armenian diaspora. The diaspora was undoubtedly influenced by Russian and European portrayals of the Armenians within the

Ottoman Empire as victims requiring liberation, while the Armenians themselves were eager to obtain equality within the Ottoman Empire.

In a manner similar to the events on Mount Lebanon, the old social structures of notables who provided the region with some stability were chipped away. The sultan used neighboring Kurdish tribes to oppress the Armenian peasants. With the help of the two new parties, the Armenians had to organize their self-defense. The deep-seated and growing sense of ethnic identity brought the parties into brutal conflict with the sultan, who did not hesitate to crush these movements in a series of massacres. Between 1894 and 1896 an estimated 100,000 to 250,000 Armenians were murdered. European newspapers and missionary reports covered these events as they did with the Mount Lebanon massacre and gave the sultan the title "Bloody Sultan." On July 21, 1905, an assassination attempt by the Armenian Revolutionary Federation against the sultan failed, and from then on, the empire regarded both Armenian organizations as terrorist organizations.[4]

In 1908 a new Turkish party, known as the Young Turks,[5] deposed the sultan, took control of the Ottoman Empire, and reinstituted the Ottoman constitution. This change allowed for a multiparty system to evolve in which the Armenian parties were included. The strong wing known as the Committee of Union and Progress (CUP) gave hope that this movement with its liberal outlook might bring real reform and equality to all citizens, irrespective of their religion and ethnicity.

Yet slowly but surely, by 1913 an extreme wing of the CUP party had taken over. Its ideology was contrary to the long-prevailing status quo of a multireligious and multiethnic empire. By late 1912 the empire had lost the entire Balkans, and little was left of its once-vast territories. To save the crumbling empire, a vision was drawn up for a state based on one primary ethnoreligious identity of which Muslim Turks made up the overwhelming majority. The other ethnoreligious groups (Armenians, Assyrians, and Greeks) were viewed with suspicion, almost as a fifth column, and a permanent reason for foreign intervention. Thus, the CUP adopted a policy of Turkification and demographic engineering. Several areas in the empire with an Armenian, Greek, or Assyrian majority could not be toler-ated. The proportion of non-Muslim and non-Turks was to be kept under 10 percent. But how to do this?

The First World War offered an opportunity to do exactly that. While European powers were busy fighting each other in spring 1915, the CUP started to deport Armenians to the Syrian desert. Armenian properties were confiscated, their women were raped, the population was put in concentration camps, and many were forced to convert. Between 800,000 and 1.5 million Armenians[6] were massacred, and hundreds of thousands ended up in neigh-boring countries: Syria, Lebanon, and Palestine. The CUP plan of the annihilation of the Armenian people from the Ottoman Empire was almost complete. Of the more than 1.5 million Arme-nians who lived in Anatolia prior to World War I, only 77,000 were counted in the 1927 Turkish census.[7]

The fate of the Assyrian Christians was no better. They lost a third of their population in the area; eight out of the twenty dio-ceses at that time were completely wiped out and ceased to exist. By the end of World War I, the only remaining Christian com-munity was that of the Greek Orthodox. To complete the plan of demographic engineering, the Turkish president Atatürk signed an agreement with Greece in 1922 for a population exchange. The 464,000 Muslim Turks in Greece would leave Greece in exchange for 1.34 million Greeks who would leave Turkey for Greece. As a result, the multireligious and multiethnic empire was no more. Turkey became a monoreligious and monoethnic Turkish Repub-lic with an absolute Muslim majority. From over three million Christians living in the empire prior to 1914, only a quarter of a million survived. Over 90 percent of the Christians of Turkey were no longer living there.[8]

This Christian genocide had multiple causes[9] that were inter-twined. Religion[10] was certainly part of the problem, but so was nationalism.[11] When religion, in this case Islam, blurred with Turkish nationalism, the outcome was a very dangerous exclusive and sectarian ideology.[12] Other socioeconomic components must also have existed. The context of the World War I provided the CUP with the cover to put this ideology into action. The genocide was not inevitable: European, and specifically German, complicity allowed it to happen.[13]

Germany had no colonies and little influence in the Middle East compared with France, Britain, or Russia. However, imperial Germany had a huge interest in the region, which found its articulation in the Berlin–Baghdad railway project. Construction started in 1903 and was to give Germany access to the Persian Gulf and to the oil fields in Mesopotamia. Germany needed the Ottoman Empire because a major part of the railway passed through Ottoman territories, while the Ottomans needed Germany to stop Russian incursions into their empire. German-Ottoman relations progressed and before the start of World War I, German officers were already entrusted with restructuring the Ottoman army. In August 1914 Germany and the Ottoman Empire signed a military alliance making Germany the main political and military ally of the Ottoman Empire in World War I, as well as the dominant partner in the alliance. Throughout World War I there was close cooperation between the German intelligence apparatus and its Ottoman counterpart. German officers were even entrusted with the army that was controlling major Armenian provinces.

Recent research has shown clear German complicity in the Armenian Genocide. German officials were very well aware of what was happening inside the Ottoman Empire and the Armenian Genocide. As early as May 15, 1915, the German vice-consul in Erzerum, Max Erwin von Scheubner-Richter, wrote to Berlin stating: "The misery of the expelled Armenians was dreadful. An evacuation of such a size is tantamount to a massacre due to lack of any kind of transportation, barely half of these people will reach their destination alive."[14] A few weeks later the German ambassador in Istanbul, Baron von Wangenheim, informed Berlin of the Turkish goal: "The manner in which relocation is being handled demonstrates that the government is in fact pursuing the goal of annihilating the Armenian race in Turkey."[15] Turkish military commanders were not apologetic about their goal and revealed their true intentions in many conversations with German officials. Vice-Consul Scheubner-Richter quoted the Turkish commander in chief of the 3rd Army, Mahmud Kamil Pasha, as saying: "Pasha openly admits that the final goal of their actions against the Armenians is their total annihilation in Turkey. . . . After the war we will not have any more Armenians in Turkey."[16] It is clear even now that high-ranking German Generals issued clear orders for the deportation of Armenians.[17]

It is not known how much information was available to the German people, but it was undoubtedly less than that in the British, French, or Russian newspapers. In a press conference on December 23, 1915, journalists were instructed by the government "to remain silent."[18] "In accord with the High Command, it has been decided that nothing will be said in the press about the Armenian issue. The Armenian Question was to be treated as 'touch me not.'"[19] This German complicity is strange when one considers the fact that Emperor Wilhelm II was not only a pious Christian who saw himself as an emperor entrusted with the Holy Roman Empire, but as the king of Prussia he was also the head of the German Protestant Church. How did the head of the German church side with the Ottoman Turks against fellow Christians? Why did he not only remain silent but allow genocide of such magnitude to take place? The emperor gave clear instructions to his generals "not to interfere in Turkey's internal affairs. This prohibition extended to the Armenian Question."[20] The German ambassador in Istanbul, Baron von Wangenheim, gave an explanation for this German stance: "Germany must be especially careful not to antagonize the Turkish government. Otherwise we run the risk of jeopardizing our goals in Turkey, our national interests."[21] When asked to indicate displeasure to the Turks over the Armenian Genocide, the German chancellor Theobald von Bethmann-Hollweg made it clear: "Our only aim is to keep Turkey on our side until the end of the war, no matter whether as a result Armenians do perish or not."[22] This shows that European powers, although of a Christian background, only used the pretext of persecution to show support to the Christians of the Middle East for as long as it matched their own agenda. Their own political and economic priorities took first place, and they would not hesitate to sacrifice the Christians of the Middle East on the altar of their interests. Even when a two-thousand-year-old Christian community, one of the oldest Christian communities, was being annihilated, they had no problem in being complicit and even actively participated in a Christian genocide. The oil fields of Mesopotamia were more precious than 1.5 million Armenians. Unfortunately, this has been the political calculation.

One hundred years after the genocide, the German parliament (Bundestag) voted on a resolution to classify what happened to the Armenians as genocide. For over a year, the parliament hesitated to adopt a resolution so as not to anger Turkey. Interestingly, it was the Green politician, Cem Özdemir, an ethnic Turk, who forced this vote. The Germans were not the only European power using Middle Eastern Christians for their own interests. The Russians, who pushed Armenians to seek independence prior to World War I, ended up annexing Armenia and incorporating it into the Soviet Union in 1922. No wonder that many Middle Eastern Christians do not trust Western sympathy for "persecuted Christians."

7

MINORITIES IN NATION-STATES

The end of World War I brought major changes to the Middle East. On the one hand, four hundred years of imperial Ottoman rule over the region came to an end, and the empire shrank to become the Republic of Turkey, no longer a multinational, multiconfessional power. On the other hand, the promise made by the European powers to the Arabs of an independent Arab state stretching almost "from the Nile to the Euphrates" was not honored. Instead, the region was divided in the Sykes-Picot Agreement, officially the Asia Minor Agreement of 1916, into a series of artificial nation-states whose boundaries were drawn to suit the interests of the two victorious Western powers: France and Great Britain. France took mandatory control over what became Syria and Lebanon, while retaining control over the Maghreb, which consisted chiefly of Morocco, Tunisia, and Algeria. Iraq, Palestine, and Transjordan came under a British Mandate, with Egypt remaining under British rule. The British not only failed to keep their promises, but the Balfour Declaration (1917) began the process that ultimately gave Palestine to the Zionist movement, thereby paving the way for Palestine's colonization. The mandate in Palestine was to establish a national home for the Jewish people. The mandate in Iraq, Syria, Jordan, and Lebanon was to "prepare" those countries for independence, while in reality they were effectively addendums to the respective colonial empires.

As part of this transitional period, Britain chose to support a limited form of Arab independence by creating "friendly" surrounding kingdoms. The first kingdom to emerge in the post–World War I era was the Kingdom of Saudi Arabia, headed by the

Al Saud family, followed in the same year, 1932, by the Kingdom of Iraq with the Hashemite family, and the Kingdom of Egypt, established by the British in 1936 under the dynasty of Muhammad Ali. These kingdoms, however, were only nominally independent and had no real sovereignty since the British continued to control their strategic interests through British military bases and foreign policy.

World War I brought serious consequences for the Christians of the region. The Russians and Germans lost ground and influence in the region as a result of the war, and their missions in the Middle East were badly hit. Following World War I, German missionaries were deported, their institutions either abandoned or administered by others, and funds to run their programs were cut.

The Russian Revolution also brought an end to Russian missionary activities that were vital for the Greek Orthodox Christians in the region. Russia's new leaders tried to sever all Christian ties to their emerging communist empire. In addition to these realities, all the missions were damaged financially by the war and the subsequent world recession. Almost every Christian denomination, with the possible exception of the Roman Catholics, found themselves in difficult straits as a consequence of World War I and felt betrayed by the European powers. In short, the promises of the nineteenth century proved to be false.

The demographics of the region had also shifted since much of the Armenian, Syriac, and Greek population of Anatolia had either been massacred or become refugees fleeing to Syria, Lebanon, and Palestine, or to Greece in the population exchange of 1925. The location of the twenty-five Armenian Protestant churches forming the Union of the Evangelical Churches in the Near East gives a clear picture of this history of displacement. Seven churches are in Syria (mainly in Aleppo and Kassab, and one in Damascus), six are in Lebanon, three are in Tehran, two in Greece, two in Istanbul, one in Alexandria, one in Baghdad, and one in Sydney, Australia. The Syrian Orthodox lost a third of their population in Turkey, and eight of their twenty dioceses ceased to exist.

During World War I the Christian community in Palestine lost 13 percent of its total population to migration. Bethlehem, a

Christian town, lost 50 percent of its populace, while the neighboring Christian town of Beit Jala lost 30 percent of its inhabitants.[1] The same is true for the Christians of Lebanon, where the annual rate of migration between 1900 and 1914 was fifteen thousand people, 85 percent of whom were Christians.[2] Most of these Christians migrated to Latin America to escape being drafted into the Ottoman army and went looking for opportunities in new lands.

By 1925 it was clear that the Sykes-Picot Agreement and the nation-states that had been created by the European powers in the region would remain for some time. The peoples and churches of the region had to adjust themselves accordingly. The populations in these newly created states found themselves caught in a dilemma. They cherished their Arab language and culture, which experienced a revival and created a form of bond that glued the whole region together. Yet, concomitantly, the vision for a mega Arab state began to lose its appeal, and attention turned increasingly to the independence of individual nation-states. This strain between pan-Arabism and state nationalism took root and became an important issue in the Arab world.

The change from the millet system under Ottoman rule to diverse nation-states through a colonial mandate was a challenge for the churches and Christians in the Middle East. From now on, the churches had to negotiate their role in the emerging nation-states within new political boundaries and in the context of British and French colonial rule. The approach of the Christians differed from one context to another.

In what came to be Lebanon,[3] the Maronite patriarch Elias Hoayek (1843–1931) was the head of the Lebanese delegation to the Versailles Peace Conference in 1919. The Maronite Church's strong ties with France meant that the interest of the Maronite patriarch was first and foremost for Lebanon to come under the French and not the British Mandate. His other goal was to prevent the establishment of a pan-Syrian unified territory that would encompass Lebanon and make the Maronites a numeric "minority." Thus, he endeavored to leverage the kind of state that best suited his vision. Within the Maronite Church there were two movements with a distinct vision for Lebanon. One group called for a "Petit Liban," a predominantly Christian state along sectarian lines covering only Mount Lebanon and Beirut, whereas the "Grand Liban" group envisioned a greater Lebanon that would include Tyre, Saida, and the Beqaa Valley, areas with predominantly Muslim populations. During these discussions, the role of Bishara al-Khouri (1890–1964), the first Lebanese prime minister during the French Mandate, was significant. Both al-Khouri and Patriarch Arida (1863–1955), who succeeded Patriarch Hoayek, saw that, out of political necessity, the Grand Liban option was the only viable one. These men understood that they needed the Sunni Muslims as their allies to gain full independence from France as well as to avoid a pan-Syrian entity. This particular solution found its expression in the National Pact (al-Mithaq al-Watani) drafted by al-Khouri and the Muslim Sunni leader Riad al-Solh, which laid the foundation for the current sectarian political system in Lebanon and which is based on the sharing of power among the different religious communities according to their numbers in the 1932 census. In this pact, the Christian heritage of Lebanon was recognized. At the same time, it was emphasized that Lebanon was a homeland for all its citizens. This agreement remained the basis for the Lebanese political system until its revision in al-Ta'ef in 1989.

A similar approach was adapted by the Greek Catholic Church in northern Palestine, represented by Bishop Greggory Hajjar.[4] At the 1919 peace conference, Bishop Hajjar strove to include Galilee within Lebanon/Syria and thus under the French Mandate. His rationale for this position was that the Galilee had ecclesiastical as well as economic relations with Lebanon and Syria. He believed that Catholic rights were better off under the French, who understood themselves to be the custodian of the Catholics in the Ottoman Empire. It is little wonder that Bishop Hajjar was active against British rule in Palestine, against their pro-Zionist policies, and later engaged with the Palestinian national movement.

The Assyrians in Iraq chose a different approach.[5] Iraq was occupied in 1917 by British troops who appointed a Hashemite king, Faysal I (1921–1933), to rule under their mandate. In Iraq British colonial officials aligned themselves with Sunni urban political leadership over and against the Iraqi Shia communities, who were assigned a distinctly separate and generally unfavorable set of economic and political conditions. The Assyrians, former mountain tribes in Turkish Kurdistan, were a recognized millet under the Ottomans. Under missionary influence and in an age of sectarianism, they understood themselves not as a purely religious group but increasingly as an ethnic group with ancient racial ancestry and thus political demands. During the interwar era, Assyrians, known as fierce warriors, were recruited to serve in the Iraqi Levies, the first Iraqi military forces established by the British to fight against Turkish incursions and Kurdish rebels. As long as the British were there, the Assyrians still held out hope for a national homeland similar to that of the Jews. They lobbied for this with the archbishop of Canterbury and with the League of Nations. The League made the protection of Iraqi minorities a precondition to admitting Iraq into the League of Nations. However, when the British announced their withdrawal and handed over the country in 1932 to a Sunni-dominated government, the Assyrians were outraged and felt betrayed by the British. The much larger Kurdish community was also demanding a homeland promised to them at the Treaty of Sevres in 1920. Giving the Kurds or Assyrians political autonomy meant the end of the "national project" of Iraq and a failure of the British Mandate. The demand of the Assyrians for an autonomous homeland clashed with the nascent Iraqi nation-state, leading in 1933 to the Simele massacre in the Mosul region, where several hundred Assyrians were massacred. Assyrians were viewed as protégés of Britain and an obstacle to the realization of an independent nation-state, although it was Britain who gave the Iraqi army the weapons that were used against the Assyrians. The Assyrians themselves felt that they had no place and no protection in the newly established Iraq. This led to the emigration of large numbers of Assyrians, including the Catholicos himself, to Chicago, and later to the integration of the remaining Assyrian community as a religious minority within the Iraqi state. The call for a "Nineveh Plain province with a federated Iraqi state" still echoes to this day.

In the interwar era, churches had to face a sectarian system marked by ethnic separation introduced by the colonial powers.[6] In Mandate Palestine, the British Mandate government reinvented an ethno-sectarian system of Jews against Arabs/ Muslims. This led in 1928 to the disintegration of a unified multireligious and multiethnic Jerusalem municipality into two separate entities: a Jewish one in West Jerusalem and an Arab one in the eastern part of the city. This sectarian approach was also adopted by the Peel Commission in 1937, which recommended a partition plan for Palestine along ethnoreligious lines. In the period between the two world wars, the colonial conflict in Palestine was increasingly portrayed as a partly religious conflict between Muslims and Jews, "an interpretation that replaced its political and economic causes with an invented primordial religious origin and conveniently elided Britain's role in the making of the struggle."[7] Prior to World War I, Arab Christians in Palestine seemed destined to play a central role in the construction of a post-Ottoman political order. By the time the Mandate ended in 1948, their role in political life was weakening.

Politics along sectarian lines became the rule in Syria.[8] The French Mandate divided Syria by identifying four main distinct "statelet" entities: Aleppo, Damascus (two districts with a Sunni majority), the Alawite region, and Jabal al-Druze. The two religious communities, the Alawites and the Druze, were recognized by the French Mandate as a separate millet. The sectarian approach was also implemented in the military. The French chose to put the military in the hands of the "minorities," which became dominantly Alawi, thus excluding the Sunni community. It is interesting that the French, known for their secularism and their strict separation of church and state, actually introduced one of the most sectarian political systems in the Middle East for their own political ends and to ensure a better grip on the areas they controlled.

France saw the Maronites not only as allies but as a type of French cultural implant in the Levant. The French drew the borders of Lebanon to suit their interests and those of the Maronites, who were privileged in educational and economic opportunities, employability, and political representation.

Britain had its grip over Egypt and tried to implement a similar sectarian policy that treated the Copts as a distinct legal, administrative, and political entity. The archeological findings of ancient Egypt boosted the ideology that the Copts were the original and true descendants of ancient Egypt and the Arabs were invaders.

In most contexts, Christians in the Middle East were aware of the colonial interests and were very active in the quest for nationhood and political independence. In Palestine, Christians and Muslims fought hand in hand in the 1936 revolt. Palestinian Christian intellectuals such as Tawfiq Canaan, Issa Bandak, and Khalil Sakakini played an important role in presenting not a Christian but a Palestinian case in international forums and settings. In Lebanon, what started as a Druze uprising in 1925 developed to become an uprising against the French with the active participation of Christians and Sunni Muslims. Copts resisted their minoritization by the British and engaged with the struggle for independence, especially within the Wafd Party. This era witnessed a strong sense of national unity between the Copts and their Muslim neighbors. It was in this context that the Copts refused the British sectarian proposal for a Coptic quota within the projected constitution of an independent Egypt. However, not all religious groups resisted this process of colonial sectarianism. In particular, religious groups like the Assyrians and Armenians who had experienced genocide had a stronger sense of ethnic identity and desire for protection, and saw the process of minoritization as an opportunity to express their voice in international diplomacy.[9]

In the period between the two wars, a majority of Middle Eastern Christians were not only visible in the struggle for independence from foreign control, but also felt increasingly uncomfortable with the foreign leadership of their churches and engaged in a process of indigenization. This is seen clearly in the development of two denominations: the Greek Orthodox and the Protestant churches.

Within the Greek Orthodox Church and through Russian involvement in Palestine and Syria, an educated Greek Orthodox Arab movement arose in the late nineteenth century and called for the Arabization of the church against the exclusively Greek hierarchy. This had already led to the replacement of the Greek Orthodox patriarch of Antioch with an Arab in 1899, and subsequently in the Arabization of the Orthodox Church and its liturgy. However, this did not happen in the patriarchates of Alexandria and Jerusalem. The Greek Orthodox patriarchate of Jerusalem is still governed by the Fraternity of the Holy Sepulcher, which elects and is led by the patriarch himself. All members of the fraternity are required to be metropolitans or bishops and Greek nationals from Greece or the diaspora. Against this exclusive Greek fraternity arose a Greek Orthodox Arab laity who were well educated, in contrast with the Greek Orthodox Arab clergy, who were not educated and lacked the power to oppose their superior, the patriarch. This Arab Greek Orthodox lay movement evolved in the interwar era and worked actively to provide equal numbers of Arabs and Greeks, in addition to fostering theological education for Arab clergy candidates. To that end, three Arab Orthodox Congresses were organized in 1923, 1931, and 1944, followed by another one in 1956.[10] Unfortunately, none of their demands were met, and the struggle for Arabization and independence continues to the present day. This interwar era was characterized by strong lay Christian movements. In 1942 Bishop George Khodr, together with fifteen other students in Beirut and Latakia, founded the Orthodox Youth Movement, a lay organization that became important in the life of the Orthodox Church of Antioch.

The culture of independence from Western hegemony was also felt in the Protestant churches, and the interwar era saw a quest among Middle Eastern Protestant Christians to unite as a native indigenous Protestant community. In 1919 American missionaries called for the United Missionary Conference for Syria and Palestine to coordinate the work of the different mission agencies and to discuss issues related to indigenization. In 1920 the National Evangelical Synod of Syria and Lebanon was formed, followed in 1924 by the Union of the Armenian Evangelical Churches in the Near East. The relationship of the Christians of the Middle East to Christians in Europe and the United States was one of the main topics at the Second World Mission Conference, held in Jerusalem in 1928. This conference marked the start of the growing independence of the Protestant European-based missions in the region, their Arabization, and the beginning of a Protestant ecumenical movement.

It took the Anglicans almost twenty years, from 1886 to 1905, to establish their own Synod of the Episcopal Evangelical Church and to achieve some independence from the English episcopate. In the interwar period this quest for independence grew stronger. The Synod of the Evangelical Episcopal Church fought for its independence throughout the Mandate years (1920–1948) without success. Not only were the British authorities opposed to recognition, but so too was the British Anglican bishop in Jerusalem. Episcopalian Christians in Palestine consequently felt betrayed by both the British Mandate and their own British hierarchy.

A similar process took place in Palestine in the German missions. Between 1929 and 1931 two local churches emerged from the German Protestant mission and started to organize themselves: the first was the Palestinian Evangelical Congregation in Jerusalem, and the second was the Evangelical Arab Congregation in Bethlehem. However, both congregations remained under German leadership. The fact that within a period of four years and within a ten-kilometer radius, two different congregations (rather than church bodies) emerged from the work of two German Protestant mission agencies shows how disorganized the German mission agencies were and how parochial was their missional approach.[11] In contrast, in 1931 the National Evangelical Church in Kuwait was established from the American mission. It is no coincidence that many of these churches and synods established within the interwar era had words like "national" or "Arab" in their titles.

For the Coptic Orthodox Church, the struggle in the interwar era was mainly between the patriarch and clergy on the one hand and the lay council (Majlis al-Milli) on the other. The educated laity of the church wanted greater rights and more say within the church structure. The struggle, therefore, was not between foreign church leaders and indigenous church members, but rather between the Coptic clergy and the Coptic laity.[12]

While diverse religious communities were united in their struggle for independence from colonial rule, socioeconomic developments widened the divide between these communities. The transition era, between the two world wars, of French and British rule brought major economic changes to the region. Under the political control of the European powers, the economy of the Middle East lost the independence that had been distinguished by internal trading, and became marginal and subservient to Europe's economies. European consumer goods soon started to flood the markets of the Middle East: automobiles, Western fashion, Pelikan pens, silverware, beer, and the like. In the cities a growing middle class emerged and created a demand for such items. This new way of life required that bourgeois quarters and villas be constructed on the outskirts of major cities along with accompanying infrastructure, gardens, and European-style architecture. The middle class itself was divided into *pashas* and *effendiyahs*. Pashas often held government positions and as a result, were employees of the European powers, while effendiyas were more likely to be on the streets opposing foreign rule and calling for independence.[13] Christians were well represented in both groups. A middle-class lifestyle became a new and important element of Middle Eastern Christianity. Western-style education became the norm at private Christian schools attended by many of the Middle Eastern Christians and elite Muslims. Students in private schools became fluent in English, French, and German, in contrast to the growing majorities who attended the expanding system of monolingual public schools. As a result, a gap was created between Western-educated Arab Christians and elite Muslims on the one hand and the majority of Arabs, who were raised within a basic system of education. This growing gap became, over time, a recipe for instability in the region.

The changing pattern of the economy, driven by the capitalization of agriculture, pushed many people from the countryside into the cities. Beginning in the 1930s, a new group of urban migrants and unemployed began to emerge in many Middle Eastern cities. Nationalism by itself failed to address this phenomenon adequately, and this facilitated the emergence of a new Arab ideology based on social values. Christians were no spectators in this era, and many of them were engaged in offering inclusive solutions to these new emerging challenges away from sectarian politics.

Michel 'Aflaq (1910–1989), a Syrian Christian born to a middle-class family and who studied at the Sorbonne, must have felt the discrepancy between the bourgeoisie and the migrant workers. 'Aflaq commenced his career in the 1930s within the communist movement but abandoned it later to develop concepts of Arab socialism, which, in turn, became the ideology of the Baath Party. For 'Aflaq, liberation from foreign rule and the fight for social justice were two sides of the same coin. For him, socialism meant the sharing of the country's resources by all its citizens. Separation of church and state was a prerequisite for the equality of all citizens. This ideology of the Arab Socialist Baath Party dominated Syria and Iraq for several decades and attracted many Middle Eastern Christians.[14]

Another approach was developed by Anton Saadeh (1904–1949), a Greek Orthodox Christian from Mount Lebanon who in 1932 founded the Syrian Social Nationalist Party,[15] and who advocated the idea of "Natural Syria," a multireligious, multiethnic, and multilingual geographic entity that included the Levant, Palestine, Jordan, Lebanon, Syria, Iraq, part of the Gulf region, as well as part of southern Turkey. Saadeh lived for many years in South America promoting his ideology within the Syrian diaspora. After his return to Lebanon following World War II, Saadeh was executed in 1949. His thoughts and party, however, outlived him.

The changes brought by the interwar era produced yet another ideology within the Arab world, particularly in Egypt. Many Muslims were unhappy with the abolition of the Muslim caliphate in 1924 by the Republic of Turkey, as this had symbolized for them a type of Muslim empire. They were dissatisfied with the different emerging forms of Arab nationalism and believed that the Muslim element in those forms was not represented adequately. For them, political independence from the West was not enough. They were suspicious not only of European politics but of European culture too. The Second World Mission Conference held in Jerusalem in 1928 triggered a wave of demonstrations across the Middle East. Muslims were suspicious of Western missionary attempts to convert Muslims to Christianity. It was in this context that the Muslim Brotherhood[16] was established in 1928. Almost mirroring the idea of the World Mission Conference, the Muslim Brotherhood established a kind of transnational Sunni and pan-Islamic organization whose ideology was crafted by Hassan al-Banna (1906–1949). Al-Banna was able to make a Salafist brand of Islam fashionable and to establish the Muslim Brotherhood as an alternative authority to the Islamic Al-Azhar University. This new Muslim ideology was not popular among the Muslim bourgeoisie or upper-middle class, but it did appeal to the lower-middle class, the marginalized, and those living in remote areas. Although the Brotherhood's ideology was adopted by many Muslims in Egypt and beyond during the interwar period, it was not until 1945 that its followers took to the streets to protest the economic crisis and to volunteer to fight for Palestine in 1948. The Muslim Brotherhood thus became an advocate for a political claim based on a religious Muslim identity, a kind of sectarian ideology with a transnational twist.

Throughout the interwar era, the Middle East was in labor. Many forces were trying to dictate its outcome: the two European empires in control, the rising economic forces, the emerging local bourgeoisie, the intellectual strata, as well as the political leadership fighting for independence. The churches were part and parcel of social attempts to negotiate a role and to adapt and resist accordingly.

An important feature of the sectarian colonial politics of the interwar era was the weaponizing of majority-minority discourse.[17] Minority treaties were an important outcome of the Paris Peace Conference following the end of World War I. These treaties were developed within the framework of the nation-state context of the Balkan and Eastern European countries. While "minority" in the European context was used to refer to ethnic groups, in the Middle East religious groups were perceived and constructed as ethnic minorities. Within the framework of the Ottoman Empire, Christianity was a recognized millet. Christians had their autonomy and were spread throughout a vast empire that did not make them feel like a minority. In the nineteenth-century Ottoman Empire, European powers claimed to be protecting persecuted Christians from the Ottoman Muslims. Now that all these Middle Eastern countries were under direct European rule, the rationale for the European presence had to change from aiding persecuted Christians to protecting the rights of the Christian minorities. Christians, but not only those, had to be constructed as minorities under threat from the majority and thus in need of European protection. Minoritization became an important tool of the British and French Mandates. Minority politics became an important characteristic of the inter-war era and gave Western countries a reason to interfere in Middle East affairs. Several communities adopted a minority identity and promoted themselves as a genuine ethnic and/or religious minority demanding separate political rights, special treatment, and protection. However, the quest for independence and the promise of a national project was strong enough to unify Christians and Muslims against the colonial powers.

8

A CATASTROPHE

The 1940s brought a major shift to Europe and the Middle East. The rise of Nazi Germany had two immediate consequences for the Middle East: First, Nazi ideology and policy drove large numbers of Jews to flee Germany and other European countries, many immigrating to Palestine, where great social and political instability was created. Second, the German occupation of France weakened the French Mandate's grip on the Middle East. Indeed, both Lebanon and Syria gained their independence while France was occupied by Germany.

By the end of the war, the United States and the Soviet Union had emerged as key players with major political and economic power, as well as vast manpower. Although on the winning end of the conflict, Britain bore such a heavy economic toll from the war that it could no longer retain its once-vast empire. Three major ethnic-racial conflicts were created in areas under British colonial rule. In 1947 British India was partitioned along religious sectarian lines to create a Muslim majority country, Pakistan, and India, with a Hindu majority. In that same year, the United Nations voted for a British proposal to partition Palestine along ethnic lines: an Arab and a Jewish state with international status for Jerusalem and its surroundings. In 1948 British colonial and racial laws paved the way for an apartheid system that institutionalized segregation along racial lines. The seeds of ongoing conflicts and wars were sown by the British Empire and would have long-lasting and devastating effects.

By the end of World War II, Britain was forced to withdraw from most countries in the Middle East. In 1946 the establishment of the Hashemite Kingdom of Jordan marked the end of the British protectorate there, while on May 15, 1948, Britain withdrew its forces from Palestine. That very same day the Jewish community declared the State of Israel, a declaration that resulted in an attack by Arab forces.

The Arab-Israeli War of 1948 was devastating for the Palestinians: 77 percent of historical Palestine was lost to the State of Israel, and 452 Palestinian villages were totally destroyed. This defeat was called the Nakba, "the catastrophe," and it marked a major shift in the region. The Arab-Israeli War of 1948 led to a further ten wars in the region, regional instability, increased militarization, and a dramatically decreased number of Christians in the Holy Land.

Of the eight hundred thousand Palestinians who were driven out of their homes to become displaced refugees, more than fifty thousand were Christian. According to the British census of 1931, around ninety thousand Christians (10 percent of the Arab Palestinian population) were living in Palestine at that time. By the end of the 1940s, the figure had risen to some 135,000, and Christians constituted a thriving community.[1] That number would no doubt have been much higher if the English had not made it nearly impossible for Christian emigrants to return home to Palestine after World War I. The authorities imposed strict restrictions on the return of Palestinian Christians who had left the country before that war, thus condemning them to life in the diaspora.[2]

In the 1948 War, 35 percent of all Christians living in Palestine lost their possessions, their work, their land, and their homes. The decline of the Christian population was quick and striking in the thriving Palestinian cities like New Jerusalem (about 88 percent), Haifa (52 percent) Jaffa (about 73 percent), Ramleh (about 40 percent), and Lydda (approximately 70 percent).[3] Almost half of the Palestinian Christian refugees fled to Lebanon. The other half settled in the West Bank and Jordan (7,000 in East Jerusalem, 4,500 in Bethlehem, 5,500 in Ramallah, and 9,000 in Amman and Madaba), thereby increasing the number of Christians in East Jerusalem and Bethlehem. In short, the percentage of Christians in Palestine dropped from around 8 percent to 2.8 percent within just a few months.[4] If the 1948 displacement had not occurred, the

170,000 Christians living in historical Palestine today would, by now, number nearly 600,000. The Nakba and the establishment of the State of Israel was a huge blow to the demography of the Palestinian Christian community and triggered a trend toward a declining demography. Christians in Palestine have never recovered from the effects of the Nakba. Much like the British Mandate, the Israeli authorities prohibited the return of Palestinians to their homes. Christians and Muslims alike thus underwent a forced migration; they were compelled to leave their land and start an indefinite reality as refugees stranded in camps and in the diaspora.

Alas, the depopulation of the land of its Christian inhabitants did not stop there, and many more were expelled in the years following the Nakba as the Israeli administration went on to destroy Christian villages such as Iqrit, Bir'im, and al-Mansura. The tale of Iqrit[5] illustrates how the newly established State of Israel dealt with the Palestinian Christian community. Iqrit was a village in the Upper Galilee. When the British and French drew the lines of the nation-states, Iqrit ended up on the Palestinian side of the Palestinian-Lebanese border. In 1948 the village had a population of 490 people, all of them Greek Catholic Christians. At the center of the village with its seventy houses was the church with a bell-tower and the elementary school. The people of Iqrit were farmers who owned 6,181 acres of fertile land that they cultivated with olives, figs, pomegranates, grapes, and tobacco, in addition to grazing land for their sheep and cattle.

According to the UN Partition of 1947, Iqrit and the surrounding villages in Upper Galilee were intended to be in the Arab State. In that sense, Iqrit was supposed to be safe. However, on the night of October 28–29, 1948, the Israeli military launched Operation Hiram[6] to ethnically cleanse[7] Central and Upper Galilee of its native Palestinian population and extend the borders of the newly formed Jewish state to the Lebanese border. Within sixty hours, Israeli jet fighters dropped twenty-one tons of bombs to depopulate and erase a total of twenty-two villages, after committing ten massacres on villagers. On October 31, the last day of the military operation, the Israeli army entered the peaceful village of Iqrit without any resistance and in coordination with the village representatives. The story could have ended here. However, about a week later, an Israeli commander contacted the village representatives and ordered them to vacate the village for their own safety, with the promise that they could return in two weeks. He suggested that they leave all their belongings in their homes to be watched over by the Israeli army, but they should take food and water with them. Distrustful of the army, the priest of the village, accompanied by fifty men, decided to stay behind and to watch over the village from a distance, while the inhabitants were transported by army vehicles to Rame, a village about twenty-five minutes' ride to the south.

When the two weeks had passed, the villagers were eager to return home, but the Israeli military would not allow them to, making their evacuation permanent. To add insult to injury, nine months later Iqrit was declared a "restricted military zone" with access denied to civilians, meaning the villagers. Losing hope in the Israeli military, the villagers of Iqrit decided to appeal to the Israeli High Court. Surprisingly, their appeal was accepted and on July 31, 1951, the court ordered the Israeli government to allow the people of Iqrit to return to their village! The joy of the villagers did not last long. On Christmas Eve 1951, the Israeli military rolled in with their bulldozers and tanks, blew up all seventy homes, and razed the whole village to the ground, with the exception of the church. The message of the military was clear: return is out of the question and there is nothing left to return to. As if erasing the village was not enough, in 1953 the State of Israel confiscated Iqrit's lands for public purposes, placing them under state administration.

This did not deter the people of Iqrit from fighting for their right of return to their village. In the mid-1960s, the villagers started civil actions including sit-ins, demonstrations, and strikes. They renovated the church building and used it for all their religious occasions like baptisms, marriages, and funerals, using the rehabilitated village cemetery for all their burials. The villagers displaced from Iqrit and their descendants continue to live near their original village as internally displaced people. They continue to fight for their right of return and demand recognition from the government of Israel of its moral and legal responsibility for the injustice suffered by the displaced persons of Iqrit, the revocation of the administrative expropriation and closure orders, the right of return for all community members to their home village, the right to rebuild Iqrit on its lands, and compensation for the demolished homes and the loss of their crops over the years.[8]

The Nakba and the establishment of the State of Israel altered both the demography and the geography of the land. It was not only Palestinian Christians who lost their properties in 1948: a similar fate awaited several of the churches and Christian mission agencies. Christian churches in Palestine, specifically the Greek Orthodox and the Roman Catholic churches through the Custody of the Holy Land, owned large areas of land in Palestine. Land acquisition and development had been important components of European missionary activity in the second half of the nineteenth century and first half of the twentieth century. This property was purchased via donations to advance the Christian mission in Palestine and support the Christian presence therein. Following the Nakba, a significant percentage of church property was lost either through occupation, confiscation, or shady purchases. In 1948, Jews controlled only 13.5 percent of the land occupied in the war, and much of the land was owned by Palestinian families, churches, mission agencies, and the Muslim foundation (Waqf). Following the war, Israel issued several laws to transform the ownership of private Palestinian land and church property to the Israeli state[9] over a twelve-year period. In 1948 Israel declared the villages, homes, and agricultural land of displaced Palestinians as abandoned property to be occupied and administered by Jews or Jewish groups and agencies. In 1950–1952, Israel issued several absentee laws that defined all persons, including their movable and immovable belongings, who were expelled, displaced, or fled after November 29, 1947, as absentees and their property to come under Israeli control, administered by the Custodian of Absentee Property. This process was concluded in 1960 by declaring the land of absentees to be Israeli land. Within this framework and with the Absentee Property Law, Israel seized several plots of land in the Galilee from the Greek Catholic Church.[10] Under the Absentee Property Law, the Anglican Church lost ninety plots of land with sixty-eight buildings.[11] The Greek Orthodox Church[12] lost huge plots of agricultural land to kibbutz developments, and in the 1950s, the church had to grant the Israeli state a ninety-nine-year lease on several key plots of land, including the land on which the Israeli parliament (the Knesset) stands today. The pattern of the Greek Orthodox patriarchate selling property to Israeli settlers and developers continues to the present day with St. John's Hospice in the Old City of Jerusalem and Jaffa in 1990, Abu Tor in 1995, and the Imperial Hotel at Jaffa Gate in 2005, to name a few.

Israel confiscated the properties of several mission agencies. The German mission agencies[13] were hit the hardest. Over 65 percent of German mission work was located after the war in what came to be Israel. During World War II all German personnel were either evacuated by their agencies or deported by the British authorities. Their premises were soon closed down. The Syrian Orphanage, known as the Schneller School, was bought from the Palestinian villagers of Lifta. Located in the thriving heart of West Jerusalem, by 1940 the compound was a similar size to the Old City of Jerusalem, with fifty-one buildings on a site of 148 acres. It had a thriving vocational school, a modern school for the blind, and an advanced printing press. During World War II, the orphanage became a British military compound. As a German property, Israeli terrorist organizations had their eyes on this compound and the moment the British army retreated from Palestine, the Jewish army was able to replace them. The village of Lifta was depopulated, and it remains the only Palestinian village that was not destroyed completely by the Israeli army or transformed into a Jewish settlement. Schneller owned another sizeable piece of land in Bir Salem, a village west of Ramleh. These 852 acres of agricultural land were planted with twenty-eight thousand Jaffa orange trees designed for export. In 1948 the Palestinian village of Bir Salem was obliterated. A new Jewish kibbutz (Netzer Sereni) was erected on land belonging to a German mission for Holocaust survivors from Buchenwald concentration camp. Chemet-Allah had another one thousand acres of agricultural land to the east of Ashdod, purchased by Schneller from the neighboring Arab village of al-Khayma. The village was destroyed in 1948 during the An-Far military operation, and the Schneller property was confiscated. With the loss of all three properties, in addition to a fourth one in Nazareth, the accumulative development of a hundred years of the Schneller mission came to an end. A thriving Palestinian community in and around the Schneller properties was destroyed, and its members became refugees. The land, school, and agricultural fields purchased by donations to support the Christians of Palestine and their socioeconomic development were occupied by the new Israeli state.

Beside the Schneller properties, the deaconesses of Kaiserwerth owned two valuable compounds in West Jerusalem: a modern school for girls, Talitha Kumi, located on the famous King George Street, and an advanced hospital. The Israelis erected a shopping center on the site of the school, while the hospital became part of the Jewish Bikur Holim hospital. The Commission on Younger Churches and Orphaned Missions created by the American National Lutheran Council intervened to save German properties in Israel but had little success.[14] Devastated after their defeat in World War II, and with guilt about the Holocaust, the Germans were unable to defend their property, and all these properties were confiscated by Israel with very little compensation.

The Palestinians who used to control the geography were now displaced and had no control whatsoever of geography or property. New mission agencies now had to be created to provide humanitarian assistance to Palestinian refugees. In 1947 the Lutheran World Federation was created in Lund, Sweden, and began work in East Jerusalem to reach the thousands of refugees. An emergency relief program was initiated to provide food, shelter, clothing, and medical care. Next only to the government and the United Nations Relief and Works Agency (UNRWA), the Lutheran World Federation (Near East Branch)[15] became the third-largest employer in the Hashemite Kingdom of Jordan. In 1948 a group of international and local clergy and lay leaders established the Department of Service to Palestinian Refugees (DSPR) that was later integrated into the Middle East Council of Churches.[16] On June 18, 1948, Pope Pius XII established the Pontifical Mission for Palestine[17] to feed, clothe, and educate Palestinian refugees.

In the Nakba, Palestinian Christians lost demography and geography, but they also lost in theology. The establishment of the State of Israel in 1948 posed a challenge to the Christians of the

Middle East. The creation of a modern state with an ancient biblical name caused considerable confusion. Huge efforts were put forth by the State of Israel and Jewish organizations to brand this new State of Israel as a "biblical entity." A prime example of this targeted branding was to call the ship that carried Jewish immigrants to Palestine in 1947 *Exodus*. Leon Uris' bestselling novel of 1958, *Exodus*, told the story of those immigrants. The book was then made into a Hollywood movie in 1960. The film was undeniably Zionist propaganda, and it had an enormous influence on how Americans and Europeans started to perceive or, better, misperceive the Arab-Israeli conflict.

Most Christians outside the region were no longer able to distinguish between biblical Israel and the newly created state. Sitting in church on Sunday, they would listen to texts talking about "Israel" and later that day would read in their newspapers about a state with the same name. This confusion was addressed at the Second Assembly of the World Council of Churches held in Evanston, Illinois in 1954. A reference to Christ as "the hope of Israel" introduced a discordant note to the assembly and was omitted after a heated debate. Many warned against connecting the modern Jewish people with the biblical history of salvation.

Until 1948, the focus of the global church was very much on the Christian community. After 1948 the focus shifted to the Jewish community. One of the first theological reactions came from Holland. Already in 1949 the General Synod of the Dutch Reformed Church[18] adopted "dialogue with Israel" as the calling of the church. In the new church confession document adopted in 1959, the church used the Zionist idea of the unity of people and land for the Jews, and went even further to describe the State of Israel as a "sign of God's faithfulness."[19] For the Palestinian Christians the 1948 War was, without doubt, a catastrophe. To describe it as a "sign of God's faithfulness" signified the adoption of the Zionist narrative and abandonment of Palestinian Christian coreligionists. The Zionist political narrative of "unity of God, land and people" and a "theological attribute to the State of Israel" became important features of Protestant liberal theologies of the 1970s and 1980s. Many Protestant and Catholic theologians

in Europe and North America were influenced by Christian Holocaust theology and adopted a kind of a liberal Christian Zionist
ideology that promoted an ethnoreligious Jewish state. It was in
this context that the phrase "Judeo-Christian tradition"[20] became
popular among Christian theologians who wanted to compensate
for a former anti-Judaic theology by stressing the ties and common values that bind the two religions together.

This new relationship between Western Christians and Jews
was based not only on theology but also race. While for decades
Jews in Europe had been considered different from and inferior
to white Europeans, in 1944 U.S. president Franklin Roosevelt
signed the GI bill, which declared Jews (and Italians) to be white
and therefore to have access to compensation, unlike African
Americans who were excluded. Ashkenazi Jews thus became part
of the white race.[21] In fact, if we examine the so-called Jewish-
Christian dialogue of the past seventy years, we find it to be a dialogue between white Anglo-Saxons and white Jews. No Ethiopian
Jews or ultra-Orthodox Jews were ever invited to this dialogue.
White supremacy and Ashkenazi supremacy became two sides of
the same coin. Palestinians, on the other hand, were not seen as
white but as Arabs, Muslims, and inferior. Palestinian Christians,
the native people of the land, were not visible in this Western
Christian theology. Just as Israel erased Christian demography and
geography from Palestine, so Western theologians erased Palestinian Christians from their theology as if they had never existed, as
if they did not belong to Palestine, and as if they were aliens in the
Holy Land. The year of 1948 was a catastrophe for the Palestinian
Christian community. They lost in numbers (demography), they
lost a significant portion of their property (geography), and they
lost the support of Western theologians. Palestinian Christians
were not persecuted because of their faith, but they were disin-
herited physically and theologically for the simple reason that they
were Palestinian Arabs. They were forced to make space for the
European colonialism of the Israeli state and Western theology.

9

ARAB AND CHRISTIAN

The loss of Palestinian land and the devastating defeat of the Arab countries in the 1948 War brought major changes to the political landscape of the Middle East.

First, the prevailing governments lost credibility in the eyes of their people, which led to numerous coups. In 1949 a military coup overthrew the Syrian national government. King Abdullah of Jordan was assassinated in 1951 during a visit to Jerusalem's al-Aqsa Mosque. In the same year, George Habash, a Greek Orthodox Palestinian refugee from Lydda, joined with Wadie' Haddad to found the Arab Nationalist Movement, which soon aligned itself with the ideology of Jamal 'Abd al-Nasir (known in the English-speaking world as Gamal Abdel Nasser, 1918–1970). Nasser, together with a group of Egyptian officers, seized power in Egypt in 1952, deposed King Farouk, and proclaimed Egypt to be a republic. The nationalization of the Suez Canal in 1956 was seen as a long-awaited success story and elevated Nasser to the status of regional hero. In 1958, civil war broke out in Lebanon, the Iraqi Hashemite king was killed, and Iraq was declared a republic.

Second, through all of these political changes, Middle Eastern countries were searching for their own identity and status within a world polarized by the Cold War. While some countries like Jordan decided to side with the West, Syria chose to sign a pact with the Soviet Union. Egypt by contrast, along with Yugoslavia and India, became a prominent promoter of the policy of "nonalignment." This was the period when the concept of the "Third World" grew in importance, with these nations gaining a majority in the General Assembly of the United Nations.

Third, in this polarized context, the Arab nations of the Middle East believed that they had much in common in terms of language, culture, and interests, and that political unity was crucial if they were to secure prominent collective power. Being an Arab was both an anticolonial statement and a mark of an overarching ecumenical identity that united Christians and Muslims alike. The hope was that this identity could unite the Arab world from the Nile to the Euphrates. On February 1, 1958, Syrian president Shukri Quwatli and Egyptian president Nasser announced the merging of their two countries into the United Arab Republic, which was soon dissolved in 1961. This short period marked the peak of pan-Arabism.

Fourth, it was in this era that the Arab Socialist movement reached its zenith. The growing influence of the USSR, the Communist Party in China, and nationalist socialist movements in Asia gave rise to the idea of Arab socialism. The concept espoused by the Syrian Christian Michel 'Aflaq, that there was only one Arab nation in which Arabs possessed the right to live in a single united state, became official state ideology when the Baath Party assumed power in Syria in 1961 and in Iraq in 1963. In this context, ideas such as the control of resources by governments in the interests of society, nationalization and state ownership, the centralization of production, and the equitable distribution of income through taxation for the provision of social services, became popular across the Middle East.

These political changes were like an earthquake and inevitably had a major impact on Middle Eastern Christianity. The quest of the Arab states for independence from foreign occupation in the 1950s and 1960s brought about the transformation of Protestant missions into national churches. In the wake of Arab nationalism, the National Evangelical Synod of Syria and Lebanon,[1] formed in 1920, became fully independent from the Board of Foreign Missions of the Presbyterian Church, USA, in 1959. Similarly, the National Evangelical Church of Beirut,[2] together with nine other Congregational churches, became the National Evangelical Union of Lebanon in the early 1960s.

In Palestine, and with the support of the Lutheran World Federation, a process of consultation and organization with local Protestant congregations that had emerged from the German missionary enterprise resulted in the establishment of the Evangelical Lutheran Church in Jordan,[3] and was officially recognized by the Jordanian government in May 1959. According to the constitution of the newly formed church, individual congregations would elect church elders who would then elect representatives to the synod, the legislative body. Those synod members, in turn, would elect the members of the church council, the executive body. The synod was headed by a president and the church council by a spiritual leader. From the outset, the president was always an Arab and the spiritual leader a German bearing the title Propst. In 1979 the first Arab bishop was elected to succeed the German Propst.

A similar process took place within the Anglican Church.[4] While the British Mandate government was not ready to recognize the Anglican Church in Palestine, the Jordanian government recognized the Protestant Anglican millet and published its name in the official list of recognized churches for 1938. On October 29, 1947, the Jordanian cabinet accepted the new name of the Arab Evangelical Episcopal Church, adding it to the official list. This process, led by the synod, failed to gain the approval of the British Anglican bishop in Jerusalem. The Anglican Church wanted to keep the Jerusalem Diocese directly under Canterbury. For that reason, the Anglican bishop in Jerusalem was elevated to be an archbishop with jurisdiction over Jerusalem, Iran, Egypt, Libya, Sudan, Cyprus, the Gulf, and Iraq. This change allowed Canterbury to consecrate the first Arab Anglican bishop for Jordan, Lebanon, and Syria in 1958. This nationalization process and the pan-Arab ideology of that time were key to the Arabization of the church and the way diocesan territories were divided.

Likewise, the Egyptian Revolution of 1952 was an important turning point in the life of the Coptic Evangelical Church. Celebrating its centennial in 1958, the Evangelical Church of Egypt gained its independence and committed to total self-governance and self-support. Following the Suez crisis of 1956, most missionaries had to leave, and the church became fully autonomous.

Acknowledging its Coptic (i.e., Egyptian) heritage, the church became known as the Coptic Evangelical Church. Under the leadership of its general secretary at the time, Rev. Dr. Samuel Habib, the church started new outreach programs to combat poverty and foster self-development. The entity that undertook these programs was registered with the Ministry of Social Affairs in 1960 under the name the Coptic Evangelical Organization for Social Services (CEOSS).[5]

The churches of the Middle East were deeply influenced by the quest for Arab political unity. The first to be so influenced were the Protestants. In 1955 representatives of all the major Protestant churches (Presbyterians, Episcopalians, Lutherans, Reformed, and the Church of God), gathered in Beirut under the theme "Christ Is Calling the Church in the Arab World to Unite and Reach Out." In this conference the possibility of forming the United Evangelical Church of the Arab East was discussed. The blueprint was the Church of South India, founded in 1947 by the Congregational, Reformed, Anglican, and Methodist Churches just a month after India's independence from British rule. The Protestant Churches that met in Beirut thought that their fragmentation into many denominations weakened their witness, especially as their total numbers were small. They also recognized that their dependence on mission agencies from abroad was unhealthy for many reasons: they did not have the power to make decisions about their churches or properties; they could be perceived by their compatriots, who were fighting against colonialism, as part of those colonial structures; within the context of nationalization, the churches could lose their properties if they were perceived as being foreign properties. At stake, they realized, was nothing less than their sovereignty as a church and as a nation. Although the idea of a single united evangelical church did not materialize, the quest for deeper unity led in 1964 to the formation of the Near East Council of Churches, originally a completely Protestant endeavor. This body was joined in the same year by the Syrian Orthodox Church, thus creating the first ecumenical body in the Middle East. The quest for unity was influenced, however, not only by the pan-Arabism of the region but also by the era's spirit of ecumenism. This was the time of the Second Vatican Council, which brought momentous change to the Roman Catholic Church. During this period, Pope Paul VI and the ecumenical patriarch of Constantinople Athenagoras met in Jerusalem in 1965 and expressed their willingness to overcome their differences, to convey regret for their mutually unreconciled theologies, and to espouse their common desire for justice. The Second Vatican Council was also important for the process of Arabization of the liturgies in the Catholic churches of the Middle East.

The Near East Council of Churches evolved in 1974 into the Middle East Council of Churches,[6] adding to the Protestants and Syrian Orthodox the Greeks, Copts, and Armenians, expanding in 1990 again to include the Catholics, both Latin and Oriental. To maintain a formal fellowship between the Protestant churches of the region, the Fellowship of Middle East Evangelical Churches was formed in 1974. In spite of existing historic tensions between the churches in the Middle East, ecumenism in the second half of the twentieth century became an important feature of Middle Eastern Christianity.

Pan-Arabism, however, had a fatal consequence for many Christians in the Middle East. The Suez Canal crisis between Britain, France, and Israel on the one hand and Egypt on the other led in 1956 to the nationalization of the Suez Canal by Nasser. Nationalization[7] spread quickly across the region and triggered a process whereby governments began spreading their wings beyond their traditional state areas of influence into the private sector to nationalize banks, railways, telecommunications, utilities, and water. This conformed to a worldwide trend, but in many Middle Eastern countries these utilities were owned by foreign companies. Nationalization meant moving the utilities from foreign hands into national hands, and from private into public control. Moreover, nationalization affected not only private foreign companies but also numerous local companies owned by Christians. Many Middle Eastern Christians in Syria and Iraq had benefited considerably from the economic growth of the first half of the twentieth century, and owing to their Western education, had become natural intermediaries for foreign companies and brands. Many of these people were seriously affected by the policy of nationalization, which was implemented largely in Egypt, Syria, and Iraq.

The newly formed independent governments in those countries adopted nationalization as a way to counter the growing private centers of power. Nationalization was also pursued to restrict land ownership, and land was redistributed. Private individuals and monasteries lost much of their property at this time. For the administration of the remaining endowed properties, known as *waqf*, the Coptic Orthodox pope Kyrillos VI (Cyril, 1902–1971) established a joint board of monastic and lay leaders.

The impact of Coptic Orthodox education was also diminished since virtually all schools, out of financial necessity, were given to the state and became so-called subventional schools. In 1974, the Baath government in Iraq nationalized religious schools across the country, including all Christian schools. Consequently, in the 1960s many in the Middle East lost land, capital, livelihood, and influence. This forced large numbers of people to emigrate.

The process of nationalization also brought with it a process of "democratization" within the churches, as was notably the case in the Coptic Church. Many of the Egyptian Coptic notables who had been prominent in the Wafd Party lost their political influence in the country at large, as well as their prominence within the church. This gave rise to a new educated Coptic middle class that was more concerned with church affairs than state affairs. A so-called Sunday School Movement emerged, the focus of which was inward rather than outward, leading to both social and political withdrawal.[8]

The overall impact of the political, economic, and social ferment that took place in the Middle East—pan-Arabism—and its effect on Christian communities has been well summarized by Ilan Pappe:

> In less radical regimes, where nationalization was hardly attempted, the economy affected the security of the middle and upper classes in a different way. In Lebanon, the capitalization of the local economy transformed both the religious as well as the occupational character of the city's elite. Once the Lebanese elite had been composed of Christian landlords and notables involved in agriculture—for instance, at the time of independence in 1943, 46 per cent of the deputies in parliament came from this background. But in 1968 the elite was very different: the number of deputies from a

rural Christian agricultural background was reduced to 10% of the total, while the leading role was shared by Muslim lawyers, businessmen and professionals.[9]

The rise of pan-Arabism had another disastrous effect on the region. In short, the multicultural and cosmopolitan components of Middle Eastern cities disappeared.[10] This was true especially for coastal areas like Tunis, Alexandria, Haifa, and Beirut. Armenians, Greeks, Albanians, and other ethnic minorities were among those who were well-to-do but, in the context of the emerging pan-Arabism and nationalization, could no longer see themselves as belonging to the region. In response to the displacement of hundreds of thousands of Palestinians by the State of Israel, Arab Jews had to leave the diverse Arab countries for Israel. Pluralism was, therefore, weakened, and the region began to look more and more monocultural.

10

A TURNING POINT

The 1967 War between Israel on one side and Egypt, Syria, and Jordan on the other was a turning point for the region. The Arab defeat of 1967 was not only a deep disappointment for the Arab world but also brought devastating disillusionment with pan-Arabism. The Arab world woke up one morning to discover that what remained of Palestine, the West Bank, and the Gaza Strip, including East Jerusalem, along with Sinai and the Golan Heights, had been occupied by Israel.

The 1967 War took place in an international context marked by the polarization of the Cold War. It triggered regime change in many countries, brought new leadership to most of the Middle East, and initiated a distinct new political era that would characterize the region for the coming decades. The first to be disillusioned were the Palestinians; they had established the Palestinian Liberation Organization as early as 1964 under the umbrella of the Arab League. Regime change in Iraq in 1968 brought Saddam Hussein to power. In 1969, military coups saw Qaddafi take power in Libya, and Nimeiry in Sudan, followed by Assad in Syria in 1970. The death of Nasser in 1970 marked the end of the pan-Arab era and the beginning of a new period.

Nasser's defeat led to disillusionment with the existing political regimes and ideologies, and the development of a more religious discourse. The religious connotations of the conflict were many. The Israeli name for the war, "Six-Day," had biblical connotations that echoed the six days of creation before the day of rest. The victory was branded by many as little "David" (meaning the State of Israel) defeating the giant "Goliath" (meaning the Arab

world). Moreover, the conquest of East Jerusalem became the
theme of the Israeli song "Jerusalem, City of Gold," which was the
hit of 1967 and perpetuated the image of two thousand years of
longing for the city. The song portrays the myth of Israel returning
to a barren land, to dry fountains, and to the Temple Mount. The
picture of Israeli soldiers standing by the Western Wall became the
iconic "religious" image of the Israeli victory.

The outcome of the 1967 War was a turning point in Jewish
history. The victory boosted Jewish religious nationalism, specifically among extremist "messianic" Jewish groups within Israel who
started to settle in the West Bank amid claims that it was ancient
"Judea and Samaria." This title was not so much a geographical
description as it was a religious designation with a political claim.
A process of Judaization of the newly conquered country soon
started with settlers building Jewish settlements on every hill
that had a biblical connection. The occupation of the West Bank,
Gaza, and East Jerusalem was a huge bonus for Israeli archaeolo-
gists, who shifted their focus to the West Bank, Jerusalem, and the
Temple. The 1967 victory was significant for Jewish Israelis: they
felt empowered and as if they were now compensated for years of
humiliation in Europe. They believed that God was on their side
and that they had the power to settle the whole of Palestine and
transform it into an Israeli state. A new leadership model emerged
in Israel of "the rabbi-politician" who replaced the more secular
politician.[1] This sense of triumphalism spread into all sectors of
Israeli society. After 1967 many Jewish archeologists were embold-
ened to promote the idea of a greater Israel in line with the kingdom of David. In this post-1967 discourse, the native Palestinian
population was seen as the Canaanites whose land had to be occupied by Israel. Some radical Jewish groups even called openly for
the ethnic cleansing of the Palestinian people on the basis of biblical passages that propagated the extermination of the Canaanites
and other native groups of ancient Palestine.

This shift from secular to religious Judaism mirrored a political shift from Israel as a close ally of France to reliance primarily
on the United States. Powerful Israel lobbies were developed in the
United States and across Europe to defend Israel and promote its

interests. In 1977, the Israeli government changed when the religious and more center-right Likud party replaced Labor, a secular Zionist party.

Starting in the late 1970s, Jewish terrorist groups attempted several times to blow up the Dome of the Rock. The first attempt was in 1978 when Yehuda Etzion acted in the belief that the destruction of the Muslim site would trigger a Jewish national spiritual revival. He and another Israeli-Jewish terrorist and expert in explosives, Menachem Livni, studied the Haram al-Sharif site in detail, stole explosives from an Israeli military base in the Golan Heights, and made twenty-eight precision bombs to blow up the Dome of the Rock. The operation had to be postponed. A second attempt to blow up the Dome of the Rock occurred in 1980 by the Jewish American rabbi and Knesset member Meir Kahane, followed by a third attempt in 1982 by Alan Goodman, an Orthodox Jewish American who opened fire on Muslim worshipers. By the mid-1980s, attempts by Jewish settlers to storm the Haram al-Sharif site had become a regular occurrence.[2]

Israel's victory in 1967 also had an enormous impact on Christians worldwide. The David and Goliath myth started to circulate among many Christian groups, not only in the West but also in African and Asian countries. Christian Zionists believed that God was showing his might and his glory as a warrior in the 1967 War. It was viewed as a kind of validation of the Bible. Not surprisingly, Christian Zionism experienced a renaissance. Anxious for Armageddon, the movement found itself boosted morally, financially, and politically by the 1967 War.

On August 21, 1969, a Christian Zionist and Australian citizen, Denis Michael Rohan,[3] set on fire the ancient pulpit commissioned by Salah ad-Din in the al-Aqsa Mosque, believing that he was called to burn the Muslim shrine so that the Jewish Temple could be erected there. Rohan, a militant Christian Zionist, was declared insane and later deported to Australia. In 1970, Hal Lindsey published *The Late Great Planet Earth*,[4] which claimed that all biblical prophecies show that the end of "history as we know it," and thus the second coming, was near, with a special place in those unfolding events reserved for the city of Jerusalem and the State of Israel.

However, it would be a mistake to think that this trend was found only among Christian Zionists. The myth of Israel making "the desert bloom" became widespread in mainline church circles. Christians from numerous European countries flocked to Israel to volunteer in *kibbutzim*. The rise of a post-Holocaust theology[5] after 1967 was an attempt to gain liberal Protestant support for Israel. More and more, the State of Israel came to be associated with divine qualities of redemption. An otherwise left-wing liberal and critical theology found commonality with right-wing Zionist Christian theology in which the native people of the land, the Palestinians, were ignored. They were replaced theologically as though they had never existed in Palestine and as if the land had been completely unpopulated, a *terra nullius*.

The 1967 War also had a long-term effect on the Arab Islamic world. Disillusioned by the more secular ideology of Arab nationalism, the Arab world turned to Islam in a gradual shift away from Arabism to Islamism. For the Arab and Muslim world, the defeat in 1967 was a traumatic event politically and religiously that left it feeling powerless and humiliated. Five times a day Muslims chant that God is great, he is the most powerful, and yet they saw their countries defeated by an enemy: Israel. This trauma pushed Muslims to revert to religion. They questioned why this had happened to them and blamed themselves. The explanation given by Islamists was similar to that of the Old Testament prophets: defeat was because of their sin, because they had abandoned their religion. "Islam Is the Solution" became a popular slogan in the Arab and Muslim world. The petrodollar gave this movement a boost in 1973. In an effort to show strength, some groups started to revert to terrorism.

The 1967 Arab defeat was akin to a political earthquake and was marked by several severe aftershocks. These aftershocks took their toll on the Christian communities in the Middle East on many different levels. The changes created a new context for the churches that differed from the era of independence or that of pan-Arabism. Church hierarchies now needed to adapt to new realities and to reposition themselves vis-à-vis the new leaders, who in many cases were destined to remain in power for decades.

The changing context allowed for a new Christian political leadership to emerge.

A new Christian political leadership emerged in Palestine after the 1967 War.[6] Disillusioned with Nasser, Palestinians saw the Palestinian Liberation Organization (PLO), established in 1964, as the one entity that best represented them. The liberation of Palestine became the new focus for Palestinians, with Beirut as their center of activity. Many Palestinian Christians found in the more or less secular PLO a platform for political engagement. Disillusioned with pan-Arabism and within the context of the Cold War, Christians could not turn to Islam, so some adopted Marxist ideologies. Just a few months after the 1967 War, George Habash (1926–2008), a Greek Orthodox Christian refugee from Lydda who had founded the Arab Nationalist Movement that was aligned with Nasser in 1951, established the Popular Front for the Liberation of Palestine (PFLP) with a Marxist-Leninist outlook. A year later, Nayef Hawatmeh (b. 1938), a Jordanian Christian influenced by Maoist ideology, broke away from Habash to found the Democratic Front for the Liberation of Palestine. In this era there was a clear shift in the Middle East, particularly among Middle Eastern Christians, from pan-Arab ideologies to Marxism. Other leading figures in the PLO, poets like Mahmoud Darwish,[7] priests such as the Anglican priest (and later bishop) Elia Khoury and the Greek Catholic bishop Hilarion Capucci, and various activists were influenced in this era by the liberation theology developing in Latin America. Armed struggle, the hijacking of planes, and guerilla fights were important features of this era of the Palestinian political struggle.

The Six-Day War with its religious connotations created new theological challenges. The Judeo-Christian branding of the outcome of the war as divine intervention and a humiliating defeat demanded an alternative Christian response. Prior to the 1967 War, a group of Middle Eastern Christians drafted the first Arabic theological document whose title, "The Palestinian Question as a Challenge to the Christian Faith," became something like a Magna Carta for Middle Eastern Christian theology. Jean Corbon, George Khodr, Paul Tarazi, Albert Lahham, Samir Kafity, and the young Gabriel Habib (later secretary general of the Middle East Council of Churches) were among the leading participants. This era was also characterized by Christian activities such as conferences, publications, and consultations. In 1968, the World Student Christian Federation issued a document entitled "Justice and Peace in the Middle East," which was the first Christian document to recognize the PLO. This was followed by several conferences focusing on various themes: "The Palestinian Israeli Conflict" (1969), "The Theological Basis for Social and Political Work" (1972), and "The Arab Christians and the Issues of Liberation" (1973). In 1969, the Middle East Church Council organized a conference called "Theology, the Bible, and the Crisis in the Middle East." In 1971, the Near East Ecumenical Bureau for Information and Interpretation was founded by the Rev. Fuad Bahnan. This bureau focused on advocacy and interpreting the Palestinian question for a Western Christian audience. The World Conference of Christians for Palestine was established between 1970 and 1974; the center of gravity for this theological work was in Beirut.[8]

In Jerusalem the context was totally different. Faced with the Israeli military occupation on the one hand and a powerful State of Israel that was in full control of the Holy City on the other, the heads of churches were placed in an awkward position. They had to strike a balance between being responsive to and representative of the needs of their local Christian constituencies, and being obliged to cooperate with the prevailing Israeli state authorities if their survival in the city of Jerusalem was to be maintained.

A different development took place in Egypt. Disillusioned by Nasser's pan-Arabism, many young, educated Coptic Orthodox turned to the desert, to the ancient monasteries of their church, for their spiritual roots.[9] These young people hailed from the Sunday School Movement of the 1950s but were now ready to take a further step, to enter monastic life, and to retrieve their church's ancient traditions in an attempt to find a home and a vocation. The number of monasteries tripled in less than two decades.

Pope Cyril VI[10] (1902–1971), a former monk, and Matta el-Meskeen were the two most important figures who promoted this monastic life and spirituality. Monasteries in the Egyptian desert became not only a magnet for young educated Copts but were also their springboard into the church hierarchy, as most of the bishops and metropolitans in the post-1967 era came from that milieu. While the larger Egyptian community was in distress because of Nasser's defeat, Coptic Orthodox Christians were able to find a degree of compensation in a monastic life. It is no wonder that relics, apparitions of the Virgin Mary, and miracles all grew in importance in the life of the church in the late 1960s.

In 1971 another monk, Shenouda III (1923–2012), was elected pope of the Coptic Orthodox Church.[11] Pope Shenouda's election coincided with a change in the political leadership of Egypt. Upon Nasser's death in 1970, Anwar al-Sadat (1918–1981) became his successor. Disappointment with Nasser contributed to Pope Shenouda becoming a popular national leader in the Coptic Church. While Nasser was unable to restore the Arab people to a time of ancient glory, Shenouda was determined to bring the church to its former glories. He was eager to increase his visibility in the larger Egyptian context and to reach out beyond national boundaries. This was highly significant as thousands of Copts were emigrating each year. To that end, Shenouda consecrated bishops for Africa and the Coptic diaspora.

A different dynamic developed in Egypt between Nasser's successor, Anwar al-Sadat, and Bishop Shenouda. For several reasons, Pope Shenouda was unwilling to support the Camp David Peace Treaty between Israel and Egypt. For one thing, Deir al-Sultan monastery in Jerusalem was occupied by Ethiopian priests, and Israel was not taking action to return it. For Pope Shenouda the occupation of the monastery and the occupation of East Jerusalem were two sides of the same coin. His refusal to allow Christian pilgrimages to the Holy Land, even excommunicating those who traveled there, was a blow to Sadat's goal of normalizing relations with Israel. In Shenouda's stance, Sadat saw an attempt to delegitimize his leadership, with the pope assuming the role of a tougher national leader than Sadat. Pope Shenouda was also unhappy with Sadat's attempt to Islamize Egyptian society and its laws, and was not afraid to protest publicly against that development. In the pope, Sadat saw a rival who continually undermined his authority. Consequently, in 1980 he ordered Pope Shenouda to be placed under house arrest in one of the monasteries at Wadi Natroun. This was concurrent with Sadat's move against Muslim Jihadists and was presented as an attempt by President Sadat to work evenhandedly against all religious radicals, whether Christian or Muslim. Pope Shenouda's monastic house arrest was lifted in 1985 by President Mubarak, who wanted to normalize relations between the Egyptian state and the Coptic pope. Pope Shenouda was, in turn, supportive of President Hosni Mubarak to the very end.

Arrangements between politicians such as Mubarak, Assad, Hussein, and the Christian religious leadership became an important feature of this era. With a growing political Islam, these political leaders went on to market themselves as the secular protectors of minorities. In this sense these political leaders claimed a role that the colonial powers had introduced in the intra-war era, and these leaders were thereby asking nothing less than total Christian allegiance to the political establishment. This deal between the "secular" political leaders and the Christian leadership continued into our present time.

In Lebanon[12] the context was different for the Christian leadership. Elected by a divided church, the Maronite patriarch Khreish, who served from 1975 to 1985, was faced with the reality of a civil war (1975–1990). His own Maronite community was divided into different conflicting parties and armed factions that reduced his authority to that of moral leadership with little political depth. The authority of the patriarch that had been won in the mid-nineteenth century was challenged by some of the militant monastic movements that called for an independent "mini" state. Maronite monastic orders developed a theology of "Christian resistance" against Syria, the Sunni Lebanese Muslims, and the Palestinians. Maronite monasteries became secure bases to house fighters, store ammunition, and fund the Phalangist Party. The patriarch's interest was to maintain the sectarian system, to keep a Maronite as president of Lebanon, and to preserve intercommunal relations. Compared with the tough stand of the orders and discourse of the Phalangists, the patriarch's stance was seen as weak and compromising, which left him with no other option but to resign. Nasrallah Sfeir,[13] who was elected the Maronite patriarch in 1986 and served until 2011, backed the Taif Accord of 1989, which provided the basis for ending the civil war in Lebanon and returning to political normalcy. The Taif Accord established a Syrian Mandate over Lebanon with a time for Syrian withdrawal. Following the cessation of the civil war, the role of the patriarch again became important as Maronite political leaders lost a great deal of credibility, being accused of serving their own political ends at the expense of the larger Christian community. In 2001 Patriarch Sfeir urged the withdrawal of the Syrian army from Lebanon, a move that restored his popularity within and beyond the Maronite community. This transition in Lebanon would not have been possible without the direct brokering of Saudi Arabia, which had risen after 1973 and thanks to the petrodollar economically and politically.

11

PETRODOLLARS

A major change took place in the Middle East in October 1973 when Sadat launched a sudden attack on Israel. The attack prompted the United States to come to Israel's defense and also caused Saudi Arabia to impose, for the first time, an embargo on exports of oil to the West at a period when the needs of the industrial countries for oil was growing at an unprecedented pace. The war ended in a ceasefire without a loser: the United States would not allow Israel to lose, and likewise the USSR would not allow Egypt to lose. The war and its aftermath resulted in increased American influence in both Egypt and the Gulf. The oil embargo compensated the Arab world for its defeat in 1967 by giving it a sense of power, influence, and wealth. Within five years (1973–1978), annual revenues from oil in the Arab oil-producing countries grew enormously: in Saudi Arabia from $4 billion to $36 billion, in Kuwait from $2 billion to $7 billion, in Iraq from $2 billion to $24 billion, and in Libya from $2 billion to $9 billion. Consequently, the gap between the wealth of the oil-producing countries and the rest of the Arab world became extraordinarily large. In 1974 per capita income in Saudi Arabia was $6991 compared with $428 in Jordan, $340 in Syria, and $240 in Egypt.[1]

This wealth launched countless large infrastructure projects in oil-rich countries that attracted millions of migrant workers from poorer Arab countries. By the end of the 1970s, there may have been as many as three million migrant workers in Saudi Arabia and the Gulf. One-third of those migrant workers were from Egypt, another third from the Yemen region, and approximately half a million Jordanian and Palestinian workers. Many of those migrant workers were Christians. While the Christian migrants in the 1950s and 1960s were from the highly educated middle class, this new wave of migration to the Gulf States attracted workers of every skill level. These migratory waves continued over several decades and made the Gulf the only region in the Middle East with a growing number of Christians, who hailed from diverse ethnic and confessional backgrounds. In the latter part of the twentieth century, the large infrastructure projects underway in the United Arab Emirates (UAE), Qatar, and Oman attracted hundreds of thousands of Asian migrant workers, many of whom were Christian. Almost all the churches in the Gulf are multilingual, multinational, and multiethnic; services are held on the hour in diverse languages for the myriad foreign communities. In all these countries, with the exception of Saudi Arabia, governments have provided land for churches to be built and for Christians to enjoy freedom of worship, as long as they respect the laws of their host countries. The migrant workers are not naturalized but remain tolerated as foreigners, some of them surviving in very difficult living conditions in very affluent countries. Nevertheless, the Gulf region developed to be the only place in the Middle East where the number of Christians was on the increase.

A major shift in the region was caused by the Iranian Revolution that brought Ayatollah Khomeini to power in 1979. The revolution ousted the shah and ended the long reign of the Pahlavi dynasty. Khomeini's vision was to liberate Iran from foreign control and to revive the greatness of Islam based on Shia doctrine. With major reserves of oil and gas, the Islamic Republic of Iran went on to "export the revolution," especially to countries with Shia populations such as Iraq, Syria, Lebanon, and Yemen. This policy ultimately led to a counter-mobilization and an increasingly bitter competition between Sunni Saudi Arabia and Shia Iran. Saudi Arabia, the main beneficiary of the oil wealth, advocated an extremely conservative form of Sunni Islam known as Wahhabism[2] (named for the eighteenth-century Arabian theologian Muhammad ibn 'Abd al-Wahhab), which it exported with increasing intensity and funding. Saudi Arabia saw itself as the protector of Sunni Islam and called for the spreading of Islam throughout the region and world. This expressed itself in the building of mosques, support for Islamic charities, and a policy of general Islamization. The suddenly wealthy Saudis saw natural allies in many Muslim movements.

At the same time, the military intervention of the Soviets in Afghanistan in 1979–1989 sowed the seeds of a religiously inspired Islamist movement supported by the United States and Saudi Arabia that led to the Islamic State of Afghanistan in 1992. With a weak government in place, ever more zealous religious groups started to gain power. In 1994, the Taliban seized control of Kabul; by 1996, it had declared the Islamic Emirate of Afghanistan and imposed strict religious laws similar to those in Saudi Arabia. The Iranian-Saudi competition resulted in an intra-Muslim sectarian polarization of the region, intra-regional conflicts, and a growing arms race.

The petrodollar brought with it the "weapon dollar" and triggered an arms race of immense magnitude. Saudi Arabia, Iraq, and Iran spent billions of dollars purchasing arms from the West to fight each other. The petrodollar enabled the oil-producing countries to buy allies in different Middle Eastern countries and to support their allies militarily, thus increasing tensions further. The 1970s and 1980s were characterized not only by great affluence but also by conflicts and wars that exerted a heavy toll on the Christian communities of the region. From 1975 to 1990 Lebanon was wracked by civil war. The harsh Israeli occupation of southern Lebanon (1982–2000) proved devastating for the country in general, and particularly for the Christian community. The seventeen-year war destroyed Lebanon's economy and infrastructure, left thousands disabled, and produced a quarter of a million fatalities. One million people (40 percent of the total population) migrated during the war.[3] About half of those migrants went to the oil-producing countries of the Gulf, while the other half went to Europe, North America, and Australia. All religious groups were affected by this migration, but Christians constituted some 75 percent of the total number. Approximately 47 percent of the emigrants belonged to the professional and skilled labor categories. This time the migration was made up not just of individuals but of whole families who left everything behind and went in search of an alternative permanent home.[4]

Iraq was yet another country devastated by war. The Saudis used Saddam Hussein to fight Iran. The Iran-Iraq War from 1980 to 1988, followed by the invasion of Kuwait in 1991, the war to liberate Kuwait, the subsequent sanctions imposed on Iraq,[5] and then the invasion of Iraq by the United States in 2003, exerted a major toll on the country, particularly on Christians. Many Christians fled Iraq during the Iran-Iraq War to avoid being drafted into that deadly conflict. Christian migration accelerated after the 1991 conflict, mainly to the United States but also to Europe, Australia, and New Zealand. Sanctions in the 1990s led 30 percent of the population to emigrate. It is estimated that of the two million Iraqis who emigrated between 1980 and 2003, one-eighth (250,000) were Christian.[6] The largest wave of Christian emigration from Iraq was triggered by the American invasion of Iraq in 2003. Under the false pretext of nuclear weapons and a smoking gun, the United States invaded Iraq and dismantled the Baath party of Iraq and the Iraqi military. This brought chaos to the country and paved the way for ISIS to take over. Over a million more Christians felt defenseless and fled Iraq to neighboring countries like Jordan, Lebanon, and Syria, while many migrated to North America and Australia. Additionally, there was substantial migration of Christians within Iraq from the north to the south, and later to Irbil. The United States, which is now eager to defend persecuted Christians in the Middle East, actually brought about the biggest blow to one of the ancient Christian communities in the region through its sanctions and invasion.

Another country that has suffered from a seemingly endless civil war is Sudan. Indeed, the history of Sudan from its independence has been marked by division and war. The conflict between North and South Sudan resulted in two painful civil wars (1955–1972, 1983–2005), while wars in neighboring countries produced large migrations of people from South Sudan to the north, especially to greater Khartoum. Many migrants were Christians. Within these eras of civil wars, three coups d'état also took place (one in 1958 led by Ibrahim Abboud, another in 1969 led by Gaafar

Numayri, and that led by Omar al-Bashir in 1989).[7] The wars in Lebanon, Iraq, and Sudan were by no means religious or sectarian wars, although identity politics was one among many factors. In both Iraq and Sudan, oil was a major factor: Iraq has the fifth-largest oil reserves worldwide and Sudan the third-largest oil reserves in sub-Saharan Africa.

Another implication of the petrodollar was the surfacing of political Islam in Middle Eastern society. This was the result of a long process in which the Muslim Brothers, established in 1928, transformed slowly but surely from a socioreligious organization into a political force. Islamist parties in different countries developed distinct approaches to the political establishment and vice versa. Depending on the context, they opted either to refrain from party politics, to participate in elections, or to resort to the use of violence and coups.

To strengthen his standing against a communist alliance, Egyptian president Anwar Sadat decided to align himself with the Muslim religious establishment. He went on to revise the Egyptian constitution to include Islamic Sharia law as the principal source of legislation. This trend occurred in many Arab countries as constitutions were amended to become more conservative and Islamic than they had been previously. In addition to revising the constitution, Sadat paved the way for "moderate" Islamic Brotherhood parties to register and participate in the political and parliamentary life of the country.[8] After the assassination of Sadat by militant Islamic groups, the Mubarak administration chose to continue a policy of "selective accommodation" that excluded militant political Islamic groups while including the Muslim Brotherhood in the political process.[9]

Although Syria followed more secular politics, President Hafez Assad also had to make some concessions to the Muslim establishment in 1973 by including references to Islam in the constitution. However, when the Muslim Brotherhood tried to seize power in 1982, Assad besieged the town of Hama and crushed the uprising brutally.[10] In Sudan under Omar al-Bashir's rule, the National Islamic Front of Hassan al-Turabi introduced a top-down Islamization policy based on Sharia law. This was geared mainly toward the Africans in the south but prompted many Christians in the north to emigrate as a means to escape sanctions and the deteriorating economic situation. This policy of Islamization and persecution created resentment to the imposition of Sharia law and a growing Christian movement. In Jordan, the Muslim Brotherhood registered as a political party and ran in several of the parliamentary elections.[11] In Algeria, the Islamic Salvation Front registered as a political party in 1989 and won the majority of seats in the local elections. When the Front appeared to be winning the general elections in 1992, a military coup dismantled the party and banned it.

The first Palestinian uprising in December 1987 presented an opportune moment for the Muslim Brotherhood to establish its Palestinian branch under the name Hamas, the acronym for the Islamic Resistance Movement. The second Intifada started on September 28, 2000, when Ariel Sharon, Israel's opposition leader, marched with one thousand Israeli police into the al-Aqsa compound and provoked Muslim sentiments by shouting, "The Temple Mount is in our hands." This gave the second Intifada the name al-Aqsa Intifada, another sign of the Islamization of the national Palestinian struggle. It comes as no surprise that most Palestinian Christians and many Muslim intellectuals were detached from and disenchanted by the second Intifada. Hamas grew over time to challenge the ruling Palestinian party, Fatah. Hamas was hesitant at first to participate in the general elections in the West Bank and the Gaza Strip but engaged in the local municipal elections. In 2006 Hamas felt strong enough to challenge Fatah and won 76 seats out of 132. Facing much resistance and a lack of recognition from the international community, Hamas resorted to a coup in Gaza in June 2007 that put it in power to the present day.[12]

In Lebanon, Hezbollah, with Iranian support, became the strongest political power by the 1990s. The popularity of Hezbollah increased following the Israeli withdrawal from South Lebanon in 2000/2001, and again after the 2006 Israeli war on Lebanon when Hezbollah's strength was celebrated as capable of fighting Israel and forcing it to withdraw. This sharpened the popularity of Shia resistance over and against compliant Sunni Gulf states. The toppling of Saddam Hussein and his Sunni-based system in 2003 gave prominence to the Iraqi Shia community, which had previously been marginalized but had increasing transnational ties to Iran. The so-called Arab Spring in 2011 gave the marginalized Shia population in Saudi Arabia, Bahrain, and Kuwait an opportunity to raise their voices and demand reforms. These developments sharpened the Sunni-Shia divide and the sectarian identity politics of the region.[13]

Sectarianism existed not only in the political arena. Before entering the political sphere, the Muslim Brotherhood was eager to control the educational systems and curricula in several Middle Eastern countries. The 1970s saw the spread of color televisions in the region, and on most Arab TV stations, Muslim televangelists were spreading a conservative version of Islam for thousands of hours per year. By the early 1990s, alongside Egypt, Saudi Arabia controlled many of the pan-Arab channels giving exposure to Wahhabi ideology to large segments of society. Islamization took over the public space. The call to prayer five times a day was transmitted over powerful loudspeakers through the thousands of mosques built by the petrodollar in every town and village in the Middle East as a sign of presence and power. No government dared to regulate the Islamic grip on the public space. Starting in the 1980s, the scenes on the streets of the Middle East started to change rapidly. This was especially visible in the way Middle Eastern women were dressing with Western short dresses replaced by veils and long, dark dresses. The dramatic change that took place within Middle Eastern societies between the 1950s and the 1980s was like that between day and night.

The Islamization of Middle Eastern societies again raised the question of the identity of the region, its states, and peoples. Most Middle Eastern Christians were comfortable with the notion of pan-Arabism as an umbrella for all Arabs, irrespective of their religion, and with the concept of a nation-state for all citizens, or of socialism as a path to equality. However, the new emerging Middle Eastern Islamic identity raised an existential question for Christians of the region. Although not targeted directly by the Islamization process, more and more Middle Eastern Christians started to feel alien at home. There was no persecution of Christians per se, but Christians felt the pressure of the wave of Islamization that was changing the Middle Eastern landscape. Christians were forced to ask themselves whether they belonged to the region, and what role and future they and their children might have. This was not a purely Christian concern; many secular Muslims were uneasy in the new environment and also questioned whether this was a place to raise their children.

In this new context where sectarian identities were becoming more pronounced, Middle Eastern Christians struggled to find the right approach to contain sectarianism. Concerned Christians saw it as an opportune time to launch a new form of interfaith dialogue. In the pan-Arab era, religious dialogue was not an issue; identity as an Arab was enough to unite Christians and Muslims. The secular, to some extent socialist-Marxist, ideology espoused by many Middle Eastern Christians did not involve an identity based on religion. In the face of growing Islamization, concerned Christian and Muslim academics and activists throughout the Middle East felt a call to combat the danger of sectarianism by creating forums for interfaith dialogue. Most of the interfaith initiatives and centers in the Middle East were, therefore, created in the last quarter of the twentieth century.

Looking at Lebanon,[14] the rising phenomenon of political Islam and the civil war gave rise again to sectarian identities. To combat this, the World Council of Churches, through the Middle East Council of Churches, had already organized interfaith workshops at the beginning of the Lebanese civil war in 1975 to bring together Christian and Muslim youth. In response to the civil war, Saint Joseph University in Beirut founded the Center for Islamo-Christian Studies in 1977.[15] The signing of the Taif agreement in 1989 that ended the civil war in Lebanon triggered another set of interfaith initiatives. In 1990 the Lebanese Islamic Committee was founded in the hope of becoming a credible partner for dialogue with the World Council of Churches; in 1993 the National Muslim-Christian Committee for Dialogue was established with representatives from Lebanon's major religious sects; in 1995 the Balamand University[16] belonging to the Greek Orthodox Church of Antioch opened its Center for Christian-Muslim Studies; in the same year, the Middle East Council of Churches facilitated the founding of a regional initiative known as the Arab Group on Muslim-Christian Dialogue;[17] and in 1997 Al-Liqa (Encounter) was launched at the Muslim College of al-Imam al-Uza'i.

In Palestine, similar developments took place. In response to the Iranian Revolution and the changing religious landscape, new theological centers evolved in Palestine. In 1982 Al-Liqa' Center for Religious and Heritage Studies in the Holy Land[18] was established by a group of Palestinian Christian and Muslim religious leaders, activists, and academics. A year later, it launched the first Conference on Arab Christian and Muslim Heritage in the Holy Land, and in 1987, the conference "Theology and the Local Church in the Holy Land." The goal was the formulation of local theology and the organization of a literary renaissance and religious movement that would contribute to the creation of an ecumenical movement in Palestine.

The first Intifada added a new layer to the interfaith situation in the Palestinian occupied territories. The first Intifada united Christian and Muslim Palestinians against the Israeli occupation while triggering Palestinian engagement with progressive Jewish religious leaders and the Israeli peace movement in a genuine dialogue. The role of religion, Zionism, and Christian Zionism in the Israeli occupation of Palestine became an important element of the dialogue. It led to the establishment of the Sabeel Center for Palestinian Liberation Theology, which began operation in 1989.[19] In 1995 the Diyar Consortium was founded to trigger international dialogue focusing on land, peoples, and identities. The Diyar Consortium became an important location for contextual theology and an international forum for decolonial history.[20] This period in Palestine was characterized by an abundance of Palestinian theological publications by theologians from diverse backgrounds such as Michel Sabbah, Elias Chacour, Jiries Khoury, Mitri Raheb, Munib Younan, Naim Ateek, Odeh Rantisi, Rafiq Khoury, and Riah Abu Asal. The newly established church-related centers in Palestine grew more vocal in communicating the untold story of the Palestinian people in the land of Palestine. They succeeded in creating greater awareness at an ecumenical level by making mainstream Christian churches in the West, particularly, more alert to the situation in Palestine. The appointment of Michel Sabbah[21] as the Latin patriarch of Jerusalem gave these movements an important public face and voice. In 2009, under the leadership of Patriarch Emeritus Sabbah, a group of Palestinian Christians from diverse denominations issued the Palestine Kairos Document, which offers words of faith, hope, and love in the midst of Palestinian suffering.[22]

In Egypt in 1992, the Coptic Evangelical Organization for Social Services established the Muntada forum to bring together Christians and Muslims, clergy and lay leaders with the aim of promoting mutual understanding and moving people of the two faiths from "coexistence to cooperation."[23] This trend continued into the twenty-first century. During a visit by the imam of al-Azhar to Pope Shenouda on January 7, 2011, and following the attack on the Sayyidat al-Najah Cathedral in Baghdad in late December 2010, the imam suggested to the pope that they create Bayt al-'Ayla al-Misriya (House of the Egyptian Family) with the aim of "preserving the Egyptian personality and identity," restoring Christian and Muslim values, respecting differences, and strengthening the values of citizenship in both religions. Thus, the concept of interreligious dialogue was already in place prior to the January 25, 2011, revolution, and religious leaders were able to address Egyptian society and call for unity when events seemed to be spiraling out of control. The election of the Muslim Brotherhood's Mohamed Morsi as president of Egypt forced the Christian churches in Egypt to draw closer together to develop a shared position on dialogue and peaceful coexistence with Muslims, and to seek opportunities for shared social and cultural initiatives. On February 18, 2013, the National Council of Christian Churches in Egypt was founded with five member churches: the Coptic Orthodox, the Coptic Catholic, the Greek Orthodox, the Anglican, and the Evangelical Presbyterian Churches.

Morsi's election and his policies of Islamization caused serious anxieties among secular Muslims, Christians, and the military. For this reason, various Coptic religious establishments welcomed the

June 30, 2013, counterrevolution and did not perceive it as a coup d'état, as it was regarded by the West, but rather as an expression of genuine dissatisfaction on the part of many Egyptians with the ambitious rule of the Muslim Brotherhood. In Syria,[24] the Grand Mufti Ahmad Kuftaro became the face of a Syrian blend of moderate Islam. In 1979 he gave the first lecture at an international interfaith conference.

The rise of political Islam pushed governments in the Middle East to define what official, mainstream, and tolerant Islam looks like. Political Islam used religion to delegitimize the government and obtain power. Middle Eastern governments responded by defining what true religion looks like as a way to strengthen their legitimacy. Islam was utilized by the ruling parties to stay in power, while political Islamic parties were propagating their definition of Islam as a means to come to power. In the 1990s, Jordan witnessed a growing interest in interfaith dialogue, leading in 1994 to the establishment of the Royal Institute for Interfaith Studies by Prince El Hassan bin Talal.[25] Six years later and after the death of King Hussein, King Abdullah II entrusted the Royal Aal al-Bayt Institute for Islamic Thought (established in 1982) to Prince Ghazi. As part of his peace treaty with Israel, Egyptian president Anwar Sadat, despite clashing at home with the Coptic patriarch, was eager to open a dialogue with the evangelicals in the United States by inviting Billy Graham to Egypt in 1975. Sadat also visited the Vatican in 1976 in the culmination of a vision to construct an interfaith shrine for the three monotheistic religions in Sinai. The grand imam of al-Azhar, Muhammad Sayyid Tantawi, became Mubarak's choice for a moderate Islam that could reach out to the Coptic Christians.

These interfaith initiatives were boosted further by the rise of militant Islam. Al-Qaida and the terror attack on the Twin Towers in New York put Muslim governments in a position where they had to defend Islam from being hijacked by al-Qaida or similar groups. Jordan, through the Royal Aal al-Bayt Institute for Islamic Thought, was the first country to issue a declaration, the Amman Message in 2005 that "sought to declare what Islam is and what it is not, and what actions represent it and what actions do not. Its goal was to clarify to the modern world the true nature of Islam and the nature of true Islam."[26] This declaration was followed in 2007 by another declaration, "A Common Word," which came in response to an address by Pope Benedict XVI in Regensburg. This time Muslim scholars wanted to defend the true nature of Islam against Christian polemics. "Rather than engage in polemics, the signatories have adopted the traditional and mainstream Islamic position of respecting the Christian scripture and calling Christians to be more, not less faithful to it."[27]

Following the establishment of an Islamic state by al-Qaida in Iraq in 2007, and as a way to represent a face of tolerant Islam and proof of a moderate and modern government, there was competition among the oil-producing countries to launch extravagant dialogue initiatives. The oil revenues used in the latter part of the twentieth century to support a process of Islamization were used in the twenty-first century to fund interfaith initiatives as a new tool of international diplomacy. Interfaith dialogue thus became the face shown by the oil-producing countries to the world as proof of their tolerant governments. In 2007 Qatar opened the Doha International Center for Interfaith Dialogue.[28] In 2011 Saudi Arabia, in cooperation with the Republic of Austria and the kingdom of Spain, established the King Abdullah International Center for Interreligious and Intercultural Dialogue, known now as KAICIID. Last but not least, the United Arab Emirates was also eager to get involved in such high-level interfaith dialogue. To that end, they were able to bring together Pope Francis and the grand imam of al-Azhar, Ahmed el-Tayeb, in the presence of Christian and Muslim religious leaders, to sign a document called "Human Fraternity for World Peace and Living Together."[29] The signing of the Abraham Accord with Israel in 2020, though it has geopolitical reasons, has also to be seen in this context of public diplomacy by the UAE.

Yet the picture is not that rosy. The oil reserves of the Middle East that should have been a blessing became a curse. They enabled the Iran-Iraq War for almost a decade (1980–1988), led to the Iraqi invasion of Kuwait in 1990, then to the first Gulf War (Operation Desert Storm) in 1991, followed by a second Gulf War in 2003 when the United States invaded Iraq. The petrodollars used to build mosques and stage interfaith events were the same that were used to destroy three ancient civilizations and to displace millions of ordinary people, including nearly two million Christians.

In contrast to the Mount Lebanon civil war of the mid-nineteenth century, Christians in the twenty-first-century Middle East were not really active players, nor were they really the target of sectarian politics. The sectarian divide developed as an intra-Muslim phenomenon along Shia-Sunni lines. In the past decade, oil revenues have been used to fund proxy wars. The ultimate goal of the oil-producing countries was to buy allies and expand their influence in the region. Saudi Arabia and Iran, and to some degree Qatar and UAE, have been heavily involved in the civil wars in Iraq, Syria, and Yemen, and in the destabilization of Lebanon. Militant groups have led a proxy war on behalf of the oil-producing countries on foreign soil. Without the active local participation of "subcontractors" in each of these countries, civil wars would not have been possible. In almost all these countries, proxy wars involving a complex web of regional and international players with shifting configurations were fought with huge losses in human capital and natural resources. Turkey, Russia, the United States, and Israel were, and are still, heavily involved in Iraq, Syria, and Lebanon. The role of the Israeli lobby in pushing the United States to invade Iraq is well documented.[30] Israel's two wars on Lebanon (1982 and 2006) left scars on the country's infrastructure and economy. The same is true of Israel's continuous attempts to isolate Iran and to destabilize Syria.

The rise of the new conservatives in the United States under Reagan and George W. Bush, with their doctrine of preemptive war, played a major role in destroying Iraq and looting its oil revenues. Donald Rumsfeld, the U.S. defense secretary, his deputy Paul Wolfowitz, and Vice President Dick Cheney were the architects of this war that was supported by Christian Zionists. They falsely accused Iraq of possessing weapons of mass destruction and accused Saddam Hussein of harboring terror through his links to al-Qaida. The destabilization and occupation of Iraq created a political vacuum. Three years after the invasion, al-Qaida and other religious Sunni groups declared the Islamic State of Iraq. The invasion of Iraq by American troops paved the way for ISIS to take control of large sections of the country and to proclaim an Islamic caliphate. This led to the largest displacement and migration of Christians ever seen from a region.

Apart from the Armenian Genocide, the only other context within two centuries where populations from the Middle East were clearly persecuted was during the reign of ISIS, which controlled a vast area stretching from the east of Syria to the west of Iraq. ISIS occupied the oil fields in this area and established its strict version of an Islamic state. Christians were given the choice either to abandon their Christian faith and convert, pay the *jizya* (tax on non-Muslims), or leave the area and abandon all their belongings. Christians were expelled, their homes looted and occupied, their churches destroyed, and their women raped for no reason other than that they were Christian. In Syria and in the context of the so-called Arab Spring, more than eighty-two churches were damaged or destroyed, six priests assassinated, and two bishops abducted. Caught in a war zone with some areas besieged or occupied by ISIS, al-Nusra, or other militant groups, nearly seven hundred thousand Christians fled Syria to seek safety elsewhere.[31] The situation of Christians in Iraq was very similar. Of 1.4 million Christians living in Iraq in 2003, less than 250,000 Christians live there today. In the past three decades, Middle Eastern Christians were not active players or the direct targets of oppression, but they paid collateral damage for an intra-Muslim sectarian divide, conflicts over oil, and a hawkish U.S. neoconservative policy. Although ISIS appears to be semi-defeated, Middle Eastern Christians are wary of wars, political instability, and living in areas marked by insecurity. It will not be an easy task to restore their faith in their respective countries and region.

12

CHALLENGING TIMES

In autumn 2014, a group of Christian academics and young graduates, supported by Muslim intellectuals, gathered in Beirut, Lebanon, upon the invitation of the Diyar Consortium to announce
the establishment of the Christian Academic Forum for Citizenship in the Arab World (CAFCAW).[1] This group (with individuals
from Egypt, Palestine, Israel, Lebanon, Iraq, and Syria), met several
times to study the situation of Christians in the Middle East, to
analyze the context in which they live, and to explore what the
Christian faith has to offer at such times. Hundreds of scholarly
papers were presented, hours were spent in discussions, and the
outcome of this work was crafted in the document *From the Nile
to the Euphrates: The Call of Faith and Citizenship*.[2] This document
outlined some of the main challenges facing the Middle East
today. Based on this document and other analysis conducted by
think tanks and researchers, there are ten main challenges facing
the region as a whole that will determine its fate and ultimately
the future of its Christians.

POPULATION GROWTH

The Middle East and North Africa region (MENA) is one of the
fastest-growing regions in the world, next only to Africa. While
there were over 100 million people living in the MENA region in
1960, that number has grown today to more than 460 million.[3]
With a lower mortality rate and a steady birth rate (though starting to decline), the region is expected to reach one billion by 2100.
The number of Christians in the Middle East could not keep pace
with such a demographic explosion; the lower birthrate among

Middle Eastern Christians and the migration patterns that resulted from the brain drain or wars, unrest, and occupation (Iraq, Syria, Palestine) has led to a steady decrease in their total percentage. Most Middle Eastern countries do not publish separate numbers for their Christian population, but it is estimated that there are between twelve and fifteen million indigenous Christians living today in the Middle East, making up around 3 percent of the region's population. The trend is clear: from 20 percent in the Ottoman Empire in the second half of the nineteenth century to 10 percent in the Middle East by the early twentieth century and down to 2–3 percent today. The role of Christians in society is not what it used to be. Their influence in social, economic, and political spheres is diminishing. Nevertheless, they continue to play a vital role in certain sectors like health, education, and nonprofit, albeit to a lesser degree than before.

The population explosion constitutes a major challenge for the region as the available resources cannot sustain such numbers and governments are not equipped to face this challenge. Population growth is felt especially in the major regional capitals. The development of infrastructure in urban settings could not keep pace with demographic growth and has resulted in densely populated, polluted, and congested cities surrounded by large slums with inadequate transportation systems, education, and health services. Since the majority of Middle Eastern Christians live in urban areas, they have seen on a daily basis how the quality of life has deteriorated with congested streets, polluted air, sea, and land, as well as rising violence and social tensions.

CONFLICT AND WARS

In the past two centuries, the Middle East experienced twenty-six wars, meaning an average of one war every eight years. Several countries were devastated by colonial wars or torn apart by civil war. The Middle East houses 5 percent of the world's population and yet is home to 25 percent of the world's conflicts, 57.5 percent of the world's refugees, and 47 percent of the world's internally displaced people.[4] By 2050, three out of four people in the Middle East will be living in countries with a high risk of conflict. The number of Middle Eastern countries affected by conflict increased from five in 2002 to eleven in 2016. The Israeli occupation of Palestinian land is the longest occupation in modern history. The infrastructure of several countries has been destroyed: Palestine, Iraq, Syria, Yemen, and Lebanon, and there is no end in sight. Several groups have been displaced several times (Armenians, Lebanese, Palestinians), and many have had to start anew several times during their lifetime. Wars do not distinguish between Christians, Muslims, or atheists. Many people in the Middle East have seen their hopes shattered over and over again and have given up on the region. They lost their hopes for peace and security for themselves, and especially for their children. Many have resorted to emigration. Thousands of Middle Eastern people, including many Christians, have opted to start a new life in North America, Australia, Europe, and South America. Emigration and displacement continue to be an open wound, and healing is delayed. Without peace, this wound will continue to bleed. Without peace, Christians will continue to leave. Without peace, it will be difficult to keep Christianity alive in the lands of its origin.

THE RULE OF LAW

There are many restrictive laws in Middle Eastern countries, but the application of the rule of law remains very weak. In countries where tribes and extended families are powerful and dominant, smaller communities and minorities may be unable to protect their rights without the rule of law, even if those rights are granted in state legislation. The same applies to customary laws that tend to mitigate conflicts without granting rights to the weaker parties. In most cases, Christians feel discrimination when the rule of law fails to be applicable to all citizens irrespective of their family or governmental ties. In the context of civil war or military incursions, it becomes very difficult for any state to exercise the rule of law. This leaves smaller communities feeling that their very existence is under threat and that they are vulnerable in times of conflict. Resort to arms in self-defense has only been adopted as a strategy by Middle Eastern Christians in rare cases such as in Syria and Iraq, following the rise of ISIS and the al-Nusra Front, who took control of significant areas of territory. The new reality brought with it a real existential threat to the Christian presence in the areas controlled by those Islamist groups and forced many Christian communities to leave their villages for relatively safe zones such as Irbil in northern Iraq or Damascus. In both countries, some Christian groups decided to create quasi-Christian militias and take up arms to defend their villages, as in the case of the Nineveh Plain Forces in Iraq and the Sotoro in Syria.[5] The number of Christians is small in most countries, and they usually constitute a middle class with the nuclear family as the norm. Within a volatile context, Christians and minorities will not feel that the state is protecting their rights and ensuring the application of the rule of law.

STATE SECURITY VERSUS HUMAN SECURITY[6]

The notion of human security gained prominence especially after the end of the Cold War when it was introduced by the United Nations Development Program (UNDP) as its framework for global development policy.[7] It was based on the realization that real security has to be more than defending state interests and territory. Indeed, often investments in the security of the state came at the cost of the human security that is people centered, comprehensive, and preventive. In the Middle East the situation was even worse: "In the decades following World War II and up to the present, most Arab states have given their prime attention to issues of 'national security,' which in reality has meant the security of the prevailing regime. With this priority, they have accumulated and stored huge arsenals of weaponry at the expense of human, social and economic development."[8]

A major challenge facing the Middle East is militarization. Five of the top ten most militarized countries globally are found in the Middle East. Israel is the most militarized country in the region. Based on military expenditure in relation to GDP, the number of military personnel per capita, and the quantity of military hardware in the region, the Middle East as a whole is the most heavily militarized region on the planet. In 2019 three countries in the Middle East spent nearly $100 billion on defense:[9] $61 billion by Saudi Arabia (third only after the United States and China), $20 billion by Israel, and $12 billion by Iran. The region is also the recipient of over half of all weapons delivered to developing countries and over one-fourth of all arms shipments worldwide. When states are ranked by military spending per capita, six of the top seven countries are found in the Middle East. The Middle East has twice the total of military manpower of the United States and close to the 4.7 million of the United States and NATO together (excluding Turkey).

This militarization comes at the expense of human security. Although some countries in the Levant and the Gulf have a very high percentage of educated people worldwide (Jordan, Palestine, Kuwait, and Oman), other countries (like Yemen, Morocco, Sudan, and Egypt) have some of the highest global rates of illiteracy. The region as a whole has an illiteracy rate of 24 percent compared with 14 percent globally.[10] The Middle East is also one of two world regions where the number of undernourished people has been rising since 1990. With shrinking arable land, the region's low self-sufficiency in staple food production is a serious threat to human security. In addition, water scarcity is expected to play a major role in future conflicts.

Income inequality is extremely high. Some 55 percent of total Middle East income is accrued by those in the top 10 percent income bracket (versus 48 percent in the United States, 36 percent in Western Europe, and 54 percent in South Africa). Under plausible assumptions, the share of income by those in the top 10 percent could be well over 60 percent and may exceed 25 percent for the top 1 percent (versus 20 percent in the United States, 11 percent in Western Europe, and 17 percent in South Africa).[11] There is a difference between the Gulf oil states and the rest of the region. It is not by chance that the so-called Arab Spring erupted in countries like Tunis and Egypt with an overwhelming majority of people living in poverty. With a widening gap between rich and poor, the middle class is slowly but surely disappearing from the region, a class that in the past was largely composed of Christians.

MANAGEMENT OF HUMAN AND NATURAL RESOURCES

The Middle East is not a poor region but was first exploited by recurring colonial powers over centuries and recently by irresponsible policies of diverse national governments. The region is very rich in terms of natural, cultural, and human resources:

> The Middle East is a region that God has blessed with remarkable natural resources, with almost unmatched and plentiful human, ethnic and cultural resources. Indeed, the area is rich with natural resources including oil, minerals, natural gas, solar energy, wind, rivers, seas and lakes, deserts and fertile cropland. It also has an abundance of historical and archaeological heritage that is open to international tourism. And the region's unique location as a bridge connecting three continents gives it an unparalleled strategic geographic, economic and intercultural advantage.[12]

The region has some of the largest oil and gas reserves in the world. Six of the ten top producing oil countries are located in this region. However, the region has been exploited by colonial powers in the past. The Middle East was carved out of the Ottoman Empire and divided along new borders created to match the interests of the European powers. Middle Eastern markets were kept captive as consumers for European and American goods. Apart from raw materials, the region has few exports of interest to the global market. While the Middle Eastern countries own raw materials like oil, most of the refineries are run by Western multinational corporations. A great deal of the income from oil is spent on military equipment bought from the West.

Often, the governments of the region are not free to make their own decisions. The United States has several of its larger military bases in this region and imposes blockades or sanctions on some countries: Gaza, Iraq, Iran, Lebanon, and Syria. Yet, Israel is always treated by the West as a special ally and receives the largest support in military aid, political support, and preferential treatment in economic deals.

However, we cannot blame external forces alone. The leaders of many Middle Eastern countries have been either incapable of managing their resources effectively or not interested in developing their countries in a sustainable way. Although they embarked here and there on extravagant prestige and flagship projects, they neglected to invest wisely in the development of their natural and human resources. From Iraq under Saddam Hussain, to Iran in the pre- as well as post-Khomeini era, to Saudi Arabia, mismanagement of oil revenues led to investment in wars and thus to political disasters. While Egypt could not manage its population growth, Lebanon was not able to manage its diversity other than through a sectarian system that sustained a culture of nepotism and corruption. The region failed to catch up with the first two industrial revolutions in the nineteenth century, the IT revolution of the twentieth century, and will miss the fourth industrial revolution of this era. Mismanagement and corruption on so many levels have been the norm. Colonial powers used to manage the Middle Eastern population by the mantra of "divide and rule," but national governments are incapable of managing diversity in a way to achieve synergy. Tackling the ethnic and religious diversity of the region is key for a prosperous future. Christians constitute an integral part of the Middle Eastern tapestry and diversity. Inadequate management of the region's diversity leaves Christians feeling marginalized, disrespected, and underutilized.

RELIGION AND STATE

It is not a secret that an unhealthy relationship between religion and state exists in the Middle East. According to a global survey of religion and state, the Middle East region ranks lowest in terms of the separation of religion and state.[13] The three main political players in the region define themselves as religious states: Saudi Arabia, Iran, and Israel. Saudi Arabia is the country closest to being an outright theocracy. Iran identifies itself as an Islamic Republic. In July 2018, the Israeli Knesset passed the so-called Nation-State Bill[14] that defined Israel as the nation-state of the Jewish people.

In all twenty Arab states of the Middle East, there is no separation between religion and state. Seventeen of these twenty countries declare that the religion of the state is Islam, while Israel defines itself as a Jewish state. Nineteen of these twenty countries forbid evangelization, and fourteen of them criminalize conversion. Twelve of these countries ban any publication by a religious minority group. Fifteen of these countries prohibit the formation of religious parties, and ten track fundamentalist leaders. Six countries forbid minority religions, and one country does not allow the practice of any other religion.

The latest report released by the Pew Research Center[15] on religious restrictions around the world over a decade (2007–2017) comes to a similar but more balanced conclusion. Although restrictions on religion and social hostilities related to religion have increased worldwide, of the five regions studied, the Middle East and North Africa had the highest level of government restrictions. Nineteen of the twenty Middle Eastern countries (with Lebanon as the exception) favor one religion over others (Islam in the Arab countries and Judaism in Israel). Additionally, all the Middle Eastern countries defer to religious authorities and doctrines on legal issues. The Pew study, however, shows that many of the restrictions and harassments were not aimed so much at Christians but rather at specific Muslim groups: Shia versus Sunni, and so on. The same is true of the interreligious tension and religious violence that intensified sharply in the aftermath of the so-called Arab Spring. While Christians represent the largest and most persecuted religious group with restrictions existing in 143 countries, Muslims are not far behind and experience similar restrictions in 140 countries. The study demonstrates that although restrictions are greatest in the Middle East, the biggest increase over the decade took place in other regions like Europe and sub-Saharan Africa.

Most of the constitutions in the Middle East assert clearly that the state shall not discriminate among its citizens. Unfortunately, if we look at the development of constitutional laws in most of countries of the Middle East, we can see that the former constitutions used to be more progressive while subsequent amendments tend to be more conservative religiously. This is true also for the public space that has progressively become more conservative and under the grip of Islamic movements. Religion, in this case mainly

Islam but also Judaism, is manipulated by both ruling parties and the opposition as a tool to exert control or, conversely, to win power. Islam is used by those in power in most countries as a seal of legitimacy. This has accelerated the dominant presence of religion in the public sphere and led Christians, as well as secular Jews and Muslims, to feel suffocated with little room to breathe. Personal status laws that regulate issues like marriage, divorce, and inheritance are still controlled by the religious establishment. Civil marriage is not available or possible, further entrenching sectarian boundaries. Furthermore, the region does not allow for freedom of religion or the freedom from religion, which constitutes today an important parameter for assessing the level of freedom in any society. Freedom of religion or belief is enshrined in the Universal Declaration of Human Rights (Article 18)[16] and reaffirmed in the International Covenant on Civil and Political Rights (Article 18).[17]

Within the prevailing context, Christians do not believe that the constitution protects them and they have to rely on the benevolence of the political leader or head of state. This does not create a healthy relationship between the political leader and the Christian community, as it can create a dependency that may cause the church to lose its prophetic role and calling in society at large.

YOUTH

The Middle East is characterized by a youthful population. Two-thirds of the people in the Middle East are below thirty years of age. Youth (fifteen to twenty-nine years) make up more than one-third of the population and number over 110 million.[18] Older adults (people older than sixty-five years of age) make up less than 3.5 percent of the population. The Middle East population pyramid is an "expansive pyramid" characterized by a youth bulge at the base and an additional bulge above it identifying a large population of young adults entering the labor force. A youth bulge usually constitutes both an opportunity and a threat. If the market can integrate the young people, tap into their potential, and provide them with meaningful jobs, then this provides an important opportunity for growth. If the economy is too small or too outdated, then the bulge is an indicator of high unemployment, social tensions, and ultimately, political unrest. The Middle East has the world's highest number of unemployed young people, at 24 percent for men (compared with 13 percent globally) and 47 percent for young women.

The Middle East has experienced a surge in higher education. Within the past twenty years, the number of universities in the region has doubled from 178 to 398, and if we add the colleges and institutes, the number reaches 1,139.[19] The fact that the highest unemployment rate is among university graduates is an indication of a wide gap between the degrees on offer and market demand. Meaningful vocational training is lacking, public sector jobs are poorly paid and are less and less attractive to young people, while the private sector is not yet robust enough to absorb the demographic growth.[20]

Twenty percent of the youth in the Middle East[21] belong to the so-called creative class, a term coined by Richard Florida[22] to describe a socioeconomic group of workers who effectively sell their ideas, knowledge, and innovations in high-value-added professions. More and more young entrepreneurs have emerged in the region over the past twenty years amid a surge in the arts, visual art, film, music, and design. In a globalized world, Middle East youth are increasingly cosmopolitan in their outlook and consumer oriented in their practice. Sixty percent of Middle Eastern youth are urban; coffee shops and restaurants are booming with young people. In an information technology age, young people can find themselves in a distant land at a click of a button and indulge in a virtual reality that makes them aware of their "relative deprivation."[23] This discrepancy between the reality at home and the virtual reality on the screen; between what is available and what is possible; between life with so many socioeconomic, religious, and political restrictions and a life of relative freedom pushes young people to dream of relocating to take advantage of the endless possibilities abroad. Little wonder that a good percentage of young people dream of one thing: emigration. Unfortunately, it is usually the creative class that emigrates, leaving behind the relatively deprived youth. This is especially true for young Christians.

WOMEN

Women are being left further behind in the Middle East than elsewhere. Globally, women's human development is 94.1 percent of men's, but the figure is 85.5 percent in the Middle East. Middle Eastern women suffer from a lack of equality in most areas of society and are held back by the intersection of law, religion, and culture.[24] State laws, religious laws including Sharia, personal status law, and customary laws discriminate against women. International reports document the systematic gender gap based on the prevalence of a patriarchal society and culture. The state in its legislation, old cultural practices, and prevailing religious interpretations creates an environment that hinders progress toward equal rights for women. The majority of Middle Eastern countries have signed and ratified the Convention on the Elimination of all Forms of Discrimination against Women (CEDAW)[25] but with so many reservations that the purpose of the convention is defeated. Of twenty-one countries, fifteen have lower female representation in national parliaments than the global average of 25 percent. Only two countries have above the average. In eleven countries women cannot pass on their nationality to their spouse or children. In family matters, women do not have equal rights (divorce, custody, etc.), and women inherit half that of men. Middle Eastern women have 50 percent less chance than men to have a bank account compared with 10 percent globally. Female participation in the formal labor force is the lowest in the world, at 21 percent, and a large percentage of women are engaged in unpaid care or domestic work. The income disparity is staggering: globally women's income is 57 percent that of men, but in the Middle East it is only 21 percent that of men. Many young Christian women feel suffocated by such an environment and seek to live in a free society abroad.

CLIMATE CHANGE

The Middle East region is particularly vulnerable to climate change. It is one of the world's most water-scarce and dry regions with high dependency on climate-sensitive agriculture. Much of its population and economic activity are located in flood-prone

urban coastal zones. Higher temperatures and reduced precip-
itation will increase the occurrence of droughts. Currently, over
two hundred million people are exposed to water stress that puts
increased pressure on groundwater resources, which are frequently
being extracted beyond the recharge potential of the aquifers. In
urban areas in North Africa and the Gulf region, a temperature
increase of one to three degrees could expose six to twenty-five
million people to coastal flooding.

Climate change in large parts of the Middle East and North
Africa could lead to a situation where the very survival of the
inhabitants is in jeopardy.[26] By 2050, during the warmest periods,
temperatures will not fall below thirty degrees Celsius (86°F) at
night and could rise to forty-six degrees Celsius (115°F) during the
day. By 2100, midday temperatures on hot days could even climb
to fifty degrees Celsius (122°F), with heatwaves occurring ten times
more often than they do now. Between 1986 and 2005, it was very
hot for an average period of about 16 days, by 2050 it might be hot
for 80 days per year, and up to 120 days by 2100. Researchers from
MIT are predicting that future temperatures in Southwest Asia will
exceed the threshold of human adaptability. By 2100 the Middle
East will become almost uninhabitable, as heat and humidity will
be fundamentally hostile to human life.[27] "Climate change will significantly worsen living conditions in the Middle East and North
Africa. Prolonged heatwaves and desert dust storms can render
some regions uninhabitable, which will surely contribute to the
pressure to migrate."[28] Middle Eastern Christians are already especially vulnerable to emigration, and climate change will take its
toll on the Christian community.

HUMAN DIGNITY

A key demand of the people who took to the streets in the wake
of the so-called Arab Spring was for human dignity. All the challenges that we have listed here are detrimental to the quality of life
of people in the Middle East and have an impact on society, ultimately resulting in the violation of the "inherent dignity and of the
equal and inalienable rights"[29] of every citizen. These challenges
affect all the people of the region: Christians, Muslims, Druze,

atheists. Middle Eastern Christians are no spectators in this region but are part and parcel of it. Like others, they are affected by these challenges; like others, they have contributed to a deteriorating situation and also have the potential to be part of the solution. Christians are found in all spectrums of society. Some are richer while others are poorer. Some stand with the prevailing political establishment while others are vocal in their opposition. For some, their Christian identity is essential while others have a more secular outlook. Christians have different ways to deal with these challenges: Some give up hope for the region, see it as a hopeless case, and opt to emigrate. Others feel oppressed by the challenges, targeted as Christians, and even persecuted. A small number of Christians may not emigrate physically but do so "religiously" by opting for a cheap theology that this current world is lost and beyond repair, and they should await salvation in the afterlife. Others indulge in a mode of consumerism and put aside other issues. Nevertheless, many Christians in the Middle East remain steadfast in their countries because this is where their national, religious, and cultural roots lie, this is where they belong, and they will not be satisfied with being less than equal citizens.

EPILOGUE

Christian persecution is a Western construct that says more about the West than about the Christians of the Middle East. It is a perception rather than an actual description, and the politics that underlie it should not be underestimated. It was the evangelicals in the United States who created the concept of Christian persecution as a central theme in their teaching and promoted it in Congress with some success. Geopolitical changes provided the framework for this development. Up until 1991, the Soviet Union was the focal point for the evangelical movement. Evangelicals were busy smuggling Bibles into "atheist and communist" Russia, where the church had to exist underground and new believers were persecuted. The Soviet Union was the archenemy of the United States and of the Christian Right. The sudden collapse of the Soviet Union caused a tectonic shift geopolitically that had a huge impact on the evangelical movement. With the archenemy defeated, the gates of Russia and Eastern Europe were wide open to Western missionaries and their preaching. This forced the evangelicals to rethink their focus and strategy.

This shift in focus was articulated at the Second International Conference on World Evangelization, known also as Lausanne II, held in Manila in 1989. Luis Bush, an Argentinian-born Christian, urged the 4,300 evangelical leaders from 173 countries to focus their energy in future on what he called the "resistant belt," encompassing Saharan and North Africa, the Middle East, and all the way to India and China. This region was coined by Bush as the 10/40 window, referring to its location between ten and forty degrees north of the equator. According to Bush, this region had the greatest poverty, the lowest quality of life, and the least access to Christian resources.[1] As well as Hindus and Buddhists, this region happened to have over 90 percent of the world Muslim population. Thus, Islam became the main enemy of the evangelical movement. In July 1992, *Christianity Today* printed a special issue on the "persecuted church" with reference to persecuted Christians in the Islamic world.[2] By the mid-1990s, a surge in evangelical writing on Christians persecuted under Islam was evident. The emerging worldwide web was utilized by the movement to share horrific stories and videos of individuals suffering at the hands of Muslim fundamentalists.

In 1996 the evangelical movement launched the International Day of Prayer for the Persecuted Church, to be observed on the first Sunday of November every year. On this day, evangelical congregations pray for persecuted Christians and donate to organizations devoted to this cause. With tens of thousands of congregations participating in this regular event, the issue of Christian persecution became a popular one and generated immense funding for organizations like Open Doors, Voice of the Martyrs, International Christian Concern, Compass Direct News, and Christian Freedom International, thus creating a sort of evangelical industry. The more Christians are persecuted and the more horrific their stories are, the more funds will flow into these evangelical organizations. For this industry to be credible, it has to have a theological undergirding: "The blood of the Christians is the seed of the church" became an important tagline for this movement.

Having anchored itself at a congregational level, this evangelical movement was strong enough to push for a hearing on Capitol Hill. Over two years (1996–1997), a total of six congressional hearings were conducted on "religious freedom and the persecution of Christians," while two different bills on a Freedom from Religious Persecution Act were circulating.[3] As a result of intense lobbying by the evangelical movement, in 1998 Congress passed the International Religious Freedom Act (IRFA) mandating the publication of annual lists of "countries of concern" and allowing for gradual sanctions by the administration. Three entities were created by this act to monitor religious freedom as a foreign policy of the

United States: an ambassador-at-large for international religious freedom with the State Department tasked with carrying out the provisions of the IRFA, a bipartisan U.S. Commission on International Religious Freedom, and a special advisor to the National Security Council.[4]

For three decades, evangelicals have driven the agenda of Christian persecution. With the help of their Republican representatives, they have dictated U.S. legislation that favors their version of international human rights with a narrow focus on Christian persecution. The extent to which this theme of persecuted Christians is an American evangelical creation is evident when compared with Europe. In 2013 the Council of the European Union adopted EU Guidelines on the Promotion and Protection of Freedom of Religion or Belief. Derived from Articles 18 of both the Universal Declaration of Human Rights (UDHR) and of the International Covenant on Civil and Political Rights (ICCPR), the European guidelines became known as FoRB: freedom of religion and belief. The guidelines mirror international human rights on religious freedom per se rather than focusing on Christian persecution, and they cover freedom of belief in general, including the freedom not to believe. Freedom from religion is something that American evangelicals, with their anti-secular agenda, would never have advocated. In 2016 the European Union assigned a special envoy for the promotion of freedom of religion and belief, and several European countries responded by appointing special ambassadors for freedom of religion and belief.[5]

The election of President Trump and his evangelical vice president in 2016 brought the issue of Christian persecution back into focus. Just four months into office, Vice President Pence addressed a gathering organized in Washington by evangelical leader Franklin Graham and described as "a first ever World Summit in Defense of Persecuted Christians." This was originally an idea developed by Graham and the Russian Orthodox metropolitan Hilarion Alfeyev. The conference was planned to take place in Moscow under the patronage of President Putin, who describes himself as the defender of Christians in both Russia and Syria. However, when

Russia announced new laws restricting freedom of religion, Graham moved the whole event to Washington, D.C.[6]

In his conference address, Vice President Pence explained that "no people of faith today face greater hostility or hatred than the followers of Christ." In the same address Pence singled out "the suffering of Christians in the Middle East," referring mainly to Egypt, Syria, and Iraq, and said:

> The Christian communities where the message of our Lord was first uttered and embraced today, though, are often the targets of unspeakable atrocity. In Egypt, just recently, we saw bombs explode in churches in the very midst of the celebration of Palm Sunday. A day of hope was transformed into tragedy. . . . In Iraq, at the hands of extremists, we've actually seen monasteries demolished, priests and monks beheaded, and the two-millennia-old Christian tradition in Mosul virtually extinguished overnight. In Syria, we see ancient communities burned to the ground. We see believers tortured for confessing Christ, and women and children sold into the most terrible form of human slavery.
>
> Know today with assurance that President Trump sees these crimes for what they are: vile acts of persecution animated by hatred—hatred for the Gospel of Christ. And so too does the President know those who perpetrate these crimes. They are the embodiment of evil in our time. He calls them by name—radical Islamic terrorists. . . . The practitioners of terror harbor a special hatred for the followers of Christ, and none more so than the barbarians known as ISIS. That brutal regime shows a savagery, frankly, unseen in the Middle East since the Middle Ages. And I believe ISIS is guilty of nothing short of genocide against people of the Christian faith, and it is time the world called it by name. The suffering of Christians in the Middle East has stirred America to act, and it brings me here today. President Trump rightly said not long ago—of the Christian church—that, "nobody has been treated worse in the Middle East."[7]

On October 25, 2017, Pence addressed another conference in Washington, D.C., organized by In Defense of Christians,[8] a conservative Lebanese American nonprofit organization whose mission is to advocate for the protection and preservation of Christians in the Middle East. Singling out the Middle East again, and in the presence of several church leaders from the region, including the Maronite patriarch Rai and the Antiochian Orthodox patriarch Yazigi, Pence repeated his message:

> The President asked me to be here tonight because we both believe, along with all of you, that American leadership is crucial to securing the future of Christians in the Middle East and to protecting all who are persecuted across the wider world.
>
> In the mountains of Syria, the valleys of Lebanon, on the plains of Nineveh, the plateaus of Armenia, on the banks of the Tigris and Euphrates, the delta of the Nile, the fathers and mothers of our faith planted seeds of belief. They've blossomed and borne fruit ever since. But now that garden of faith, generations in the making, is under threat. It's under threat of persecution and mistreatment. Many of the Christian communities that first embraced the message of Christ are today the targets of unspeakable acts of violence and atrocity. . . .
>
> As evidence, President Trump has nominated a great leader and a great man of faith to be our Ambassador-at-Large for International Religious Freedom, Governor Sam Brownback. In fact, President Trump has directed me to go to the Middle East in late December. And I promise you one of the messages that I will bring on the President's behalf to leaders across the region is that now is the time to bring an end to the persecution of Christians and all religious minorities. [Applause]
>
> Our fellow Christians and all who are persecuted in the Middle East should not have to rely on multinational institutions when America can help them directly. And tonight, it is my privilege to announce that President Trump has ordered the State Department to stop funding ineffective relief efforts by the United Nations. And from this day forward, America will provide support directly to persecuted communities through USAID. We will no longer rely on the United Nations alone to assist persecuted Christians and minorities in the wake of genocide and the atrocities of terrorist groups. The United States will work hand-in-hand from this day forward with faith-based groups and private

organizations to help those who are persecuted for their faith. This is the moment. Now is the time. And America will support these people in their hour of need.[9]

On February 5, 2020, the United States State Department released the Declaration of Principles for the Religious Freedom Alliance signed by twenty-seven countries, including Albania, Austria, Bosnia and Herzegovina, Brazil, Bulgaria, Colombia, Croatia, Czech Republic, Estonia, Gambia, Georgia, Greece, Hungary, Israel, Kosovo, Latvia, Lithuania, Malta, Netherlands, Senegal, Slovakia, Slovenia, Togo, Ukraine, and the United Kingdom.[10] Interestingly, most of the countries that joined this alliance were either Eastern European countries or countries with populist and right-wing conservative governments. While the freedom of religion agenda was widened to include persecuted people of other religions, it did not comprise freedom of belief or freedom from religion. Yet, with this alliance, religious freedom and the defense of persecuted Christians (and others) have become an instrument of international diplomacy.

The persecution of Christians of the Middle East has been a recurring theme in Anglo-Saxon discourse from Churchill in the mid-nineteenth century all the way to Vice President Pence in the twenty-first century. From the civil war on Mount Lebanon in 1860 to the Christians persecuted under ISIS, the concept of persecution has been a tool of public diplomacy and international politics. The pattern throughout is clear: Christians of the Middle East are victims of Islamic persecution. This discourse is part of an orientalist perception that persists in framing the Middle East as a backward, barbaric, and intolerant region with long-standing sectarian conflicts: between Christians and Muslims, between Arabs and Jews, and between Sunni and Shia. The fact that the Middle East has, for more than nineteen centuries, been one of the most diverse regions in the world—religiously, ethnically, and culturally—is ignored. The Middle East did not have one single church with a monopoly over salvation as the West did. From the outset, Christianity was pluralistic in nature. The same is true of the many different faces of Islam in the region. All these religions, sects, and ethnicities were able to coexist, not without challenges, but it was possible for the past fourteen hundred years within the framework of Islam. In most cases, albeit with a few exceptions, Middle Eastern Islam proved tolerant toward Christians even if it stopped short of granting them full equality.

Nevertheless, the dominant discourse among evangelical Christians continues to portray Islam as a violent religion that persistently persecutes Christians. In this discourse, the Christians of the Middle East are mere victims that lack any say or powers and are entirely dependent on the West to rescue them. Middle Eastern Christians are victimized, objectivized, and minoritized by their "sisters and brother" in the evangelical community. What this study shows is that this is a Western perception rather than a factual description of the reality on the ground. Such a discourse says more about the West than about Middle Eastern Christians and is intended to make the West feel superior as a "civilized" continent compared with the savage Middle East. In reality, this discourse has another important function. It was in a context of colonialism and with the pretext of protecting persecuted Christians that the European powers assumed the right to interfere in the Ottoman Empire. Following World War I, "protecting minorities" became a tool of international diplomacy. Under the label of religious freedom, the Trump administration imposes sanctions against countries that oppose its policies. When countries like China, Russia, North Korea, Iran, Syria, Saudi Arabia, and Pakistan appear in tier one as countries that violate religious freedom, it becomes clear that politics is a major force behind the rhetoric. The narrative of Christian persecution is not only in foreign policy but is linked closely to internal U.S. politics. It represents an attempt to restore religion in an increasingly secular society by emphasizing a "Christian America" that is the ultimate defender of Christianity worldwide. A dispensationalist interpretation of biblical prophecy has resulted in blind support for the State of Israel and antagonistic feelings toward the Arab-Islamic world.

The well-known Palestinian poet Mahmoud Darwish wrote a poem under the title "They Would Love to See Me Dead."[11] This poem referred to the Arab world that portrays Palestinians as martyrs; the bestselling picture of a Palestinian in the Arab world is that of a Palestinian killed by Israeli occupation forces. In the same way, we can say that evangelical Christians love to see Middle Eastern Christians persecuted and killed by Muslim violence. Such a story sells well with the base of the Christian Right; it serves conservative Christian organizations as a proven tool for fundraising; it helps some Middle Eastern Christians who target support (especially financial help) from conservative Christian organizations; it fits the agenda of some Middle Eastern Christians who have emigrated to the West and may feel guilt about abandoning their coreligionists in the Middle East, so adopt the same justification of persecuted Christians; and last but not least, it feeds into Israeli propaganda that portrays Israel as a location where Christians are protected.

As this study shows clearly, Western empires were never really interested in the Middle Eastern Christians but sought a pretext to promote their imperial interests. Over and over again, Middle Eastern Christians were sacrificed on the altar of Western national interests. This was the case with Britain and the Assyrians in Iraq; with Germany in the Armenian Genocide; with Britain in Palestine; and with the United States in Iraq and Syria. In most cases, the West was part of the problem for Middle Eastern Christianity and not part of the solution. I am not aware of a single case in which Western empires played a constructive role in creating a political framework in the Middle East where Christians and others could thrive. Even when France crafted Lebanon in the aftermath of World War 1, it did so within its larger colonial project in which the Maronites were simply one small piece of a larger puzzle.

It is, therefore, imperative when talking about the persecution of Middle Eastern Christians to look at the larger geopolitical picture. The only two cases of Christian persecution in the past two centuries must be interpreted within the context of Western imperial penetration. The collapse of the Ottoman Empire and European colonial interference in the early twentieth century were the context to the Armenian Genocide. In the twenty-first century, the U.S. invasion of Iraq, with the subsequent collapse of the nation-state and sovereignty, is the context for Christian oppression under ISIS in Iraq and Syria. In the wake of World War I, the colonial powers created problems by dividing the region up for their own economic and political interests, and preventing the emergence of a viable political structure in larger Syria. The implanting, backing, and arming of a Jewish state, the invasion of Iraq, and destruction of Syria are all part of this European colonial project. Middle Eastern Christians were victims of Euro-American colonialism and the consequences have made life more difficult for Christians ever since.

The discourse of Christian persecution is a highly selective conservative Christian theme. The status of Christian communities in the Middle East depends on a series of sociopolitical and economic challenges that face the region as a whole. It is not possible to consider the situation of Christians outside the more general context, one that is marked by the absence of modernity, political accountability or economic stability. The current overemphasis on religious freedom is a very narrow understanding of human rights. Looking at the immense challenges facing a region in turmoil, challenged by colonial history, population explosion, high unemployment, mismanagement, weakened human security, outdated educational structures, and climate change, religious freedom sounds like a luxury. While freedom of religion and freedom from religion are important features of a healthy relationship between religion and the state, they should not be the main agenda driving politics. Ultimately, "one lives not on the freedom of religion alone."

The problems facing the region today are accumulative and have, therefore, become chronic. The explosion at the Beirut port in August 2020 exposed the accumulated corruption resulting from a decades-long sectarian system in Lebanon. The ongoing Israeli occupation of Palestinian land and people has resulted in the structural deformation of Palestinian society. Chronic underdevelopment in Egypt, challenged by overpopulation and limited resources, will continue to put pressure on Egyptian society under the rule of military generals. Destroyed infrastructure, limited sovereignty, and a one-party system with little credibility will not be able to restore political stability to Syria. A rich country like Iraq has been torn by decade-long wars, sectarian conflicts, and colonial interests over oil, requiring years to rehabilitate. Jordan, once known for its relative stability, has become increasingly vulnerable. In all these countries, including Israel, there is a lack of political accountability or inclusive social structures. In many of these countries, exclusive Islamist and Jihadi groups often target Christians as pawns in their fight against the political establishment. In almost all these countries, proxy wars involving a complex web of regional and international players, with shifting configurations, are fought with huge losses in human capital and natural resources. Most of these countries, with the exception of Israel, experience multiple Western pressures and sanctions. The combination of these problems results in de-development. Under such conditions, the survival of the Christian community will continue to be a challenge.

The future of Middle Eastern Christianity depends very much on this larger context. However, churches themselves play an important role. Churches in the Middle East are not much better off than their countries. To a large extent, they mirror their societies with an aging leadership that lacks vision, out-of-date structures requiring urgent reform, and theologies that are irrelevant to the real needs of the community. The political elite of the Middle East at large have not been up to the challenges they face and have failed to create an environment in which their people can thrive. They are part of the problem, but only they can work on the solution. It is up to the people of the Middle East, whether Christians, Muslims, Jews, or atheists, to shape the future they want. This is not an easy task at all. The odds are immense and not to be underestimated. Yet the answer is to get engaged in building a different future for all. There is no future for the Christians of the Middle East without a system of good governance, a fair social contract, and sustainable economic development: these are all vital ingredients for peace. There is no future for Christians without a future for all. Conversely, a continuous Christian presence in the Middle East is crucial to maintain the pluralistic character of the region. Without a Christian presence, the Middle East will become monoreligious, monocultural, and thus, poorer in every aspect.

Many Middle Eastern Christians throughout history have understood that they have no other option but to get involved in the national and regional struggle toward social and political transformation. The history of Middle Eastern Christians is, therefore, not so much one of persecution but one of resilience, and this should be acknowledged. Over a period of two millennia, Middle Eastern Christianity survived one empire after the other by developing great elasticity in adjusting to changing contexts. Christians learned how to survive atrocities and how to resist creatively while maintaining a dynamic identity. It is obvious today that the visibility and vitality of Middle Eastern Christianity are no longer what they once were. Numbers have dwindled to a historic low of 3 percent today. Nevertheless, this has not deterred Christians from contributing to their communities and advocating for neighborly relationships, equal citizenship, and open, tolerant, and pluralistic societies. It is true that emigration continues to exact a toll on Middle Eastern Christianity. Yet, even when Middle Eastern Christians were displaced or migrated, they succeeded in developing diasporic and hybrid identities. The Maronite diaspora in the United States, France, Latin America, and some African countries is estimated to number from four to five million. Over half a million Latin Americans with Palestinian roots live as fourth- or fifth-generation Palestinians in Latin America alone, with over half of them in Chile, where they comprise 3 percent of the population. The Syrian Orthodox community, which was almost eradicated from Turkey, has survived today in several major cities, and a large Syriac population resides in Sweden. While there is only a remnant Assyrian Christian community in Iraq, many have found new homes in Chicago, California, and Michigan. Today the Coptic Church has dioceses and centers serving several million Copts in Western Europe, the United States, Canada, and Australia. The Armenians who lost their homes in eastern Turkey number around three million in Armenia, with seven million scattered all over the world in a vibrant transnational community concentrated in Russia, the United States, and France. That is a story of resilience to celebrate.

The statement of the Christian Academic Forum for Citizenship in the Arab World, published in 2014 under the title *From the Nile to the Euphrates: The Call of Faith and Citizenship*, is a good expression of contemporary resilient Christian faith with a socio-political commitment.

> We believe in One God, who created the universe and honored humankind, even making humans his vicegerents on earth, entrusting them to maintain and embellish this planet. Therefore, we are committed to caring for creation and to the responsible management of the earth's resources, as faithful stewards. We are also committed to guarding the dignity of all humankind, regardless of gender, ethnicity, religion or belief.
>
> We believe in the One Triune God. Therefore, we are committed to working towards the unity and integrity of each of our nations and the harmony of its visions and goals. We do this while celebrating and preserving the rich and unique diversity in our countries.
>
> We believe in God, omnipotent and all merciful, creator and sustainer of the universe, who did not abandon this world but is still active, creatively giving life and renewing it. Therefore, we are committed to remaining in our homelands and to being involved actively in their renewal and development, dedicating our gifts to creativity and innovation.
>
> We believe in Jesus Christ, the incarnate Word of God, who dwelt among us, who taught, healed and went about doing good, calling all peoples to repentance and righteousness, and proclaiming liberty and goodness. Therefore, we are committed to following his path, and to continuing his mission in the service of humanity through the ministries of education, healing, development, culture and the arts. We do this as we also pursue justice, seek and make peace, and advocate human rights in our Arab context.
>
> We believe in Jesus Christ who died on the cross and in the victory of his resurrection. He experienced the agony and hardships of human life, endured humiliation, and suffered the pain of injustice and persecution. He then rose triumphantly, proclaiming the dawn of a new era. Therefore, we are committed to solidarity with those who are crushed,

weak, and oppressed. We shall not give in to despair or to the logic of death; but will live with the power and hope of the resurrection, and in our conduct shall bear witness to the sanctity of life.

We believe in the Holy Spirit who works in us and through us, comforting us in our hardships, reviving and renewing our strengths. Therefore, we are committed to striving towards the renewal of our societies and their institutions, and will seek a humanity and a spirituality that enrich life and glorify its Giver.

We believe in one holy catholic and apostolic Church. Therefore, we are committed to the ecumenical spirit and to ecumenical work, to thinking, planning and acting together. We also extend our hands to our neighbors of other faiths, in order together to build just, secure, and free societies that embrace all their citizens.

We believe in the forgiveness of sins, and realize that we are often part of the problem instead of being part of the solution. Therefore, we are committed to accountability and self-correction, and to forgiving others as we have been forgiven, so that we may be part of establishing a new era for the peoples of this region.

We believe in God, the Supreme Judge, before whom we all shall stand one day to give an account for our lives. Therefore, we are committed to work diligently to assure that our countries have just constitutions, upright governments and fair laws. We dedicate ourselves to the task of ensuring that all citizens, without exception, have equal rights and obligations.

We believe in eternal life, and realize that people in our region believe in life after death, but are starting to despair of the possibility of life with dignity before death. Therefore, we are committed to strive toward ensuring a decent life for people in our time and place. As we live through these difficult times in the history of our region, when Christians are suffering from persecution, demonization, and forced displacement, we realize that this calamity does not target just Christians, but countries as a whole. We also realize that there is no salvation in sight, nor will deliverance come effortlessly. It will come only as a result of a difficult process of labor pains—as in childbirth—and through a continuing and cumulative cultivation of awareness leading to a radical reformation of systems and mindsets, over many generations.

Despite all the difficult challenges, we are committed to remaining and persevering with those who share our concerns, through the process of awakening that our societies need. We are accountable before God, to acknowledge his commandment of seeking the good and well-being of our homelands, as we have a stake in their future. This is our understanding and declaration of a conscientious and active faith, positive involvement, and active participation. Therefore . . . We believe and commit.[12]

Evangelical Christians and Western political forces want to frame the story of the Middle Eastern Christians as one simply of persecution. This study clearly demonstrates that the story is one of struggle, resistance, social involvement, and resilience.

NOTES

INTRODUCTION

1 Mitri Raheb, ed., *Shifting Identities: Changes in the Social, Political, and Religious Structures in the Arab World* (Bethlehem: Diyar, 2016).
2 Mitri Raheb, *Faith in the Face of Empire: The Bible through Palestinian Eyes* (Maryknoll, N.Y.: Orbis, 2014).
3 Ussama Makdisi, *The Culture of Sectarianism* (Berkeley: University of California Press, 2000).
4 Ussama Makdisi, *Age of Coexistence: The Ecumenical Frame and the Making of the Modern Arab World* (Oakland: University of California Press, 2019).
5 Rashid Khalidi, *The Hundred Years' War on Palestine: A History of Settler Colonialism and Resistance, 1917–2017* (New York: Metropolitan Books, 2020).
6 Laura Robson, ed., *Minorities and the Modern Arab World: New Perspectives*, repr. ed. (Syracuse, N.Y.: Syracuse University Press, 2016).
7 Laura Robson, *States of Separation: Transfer, Partition, and the Making of the Modern Middle East* (Oakland: University of California Press, 2017).
8 Heather J. Sharkey, *A History of Muslims, Christians, and Jews in the Middle East* (Cambridge: Cambridge University Press, 2017).

1 UNDER OTTOMAN RULE

1 Youssef Courbage and Philippe Fargues, *Christians and Jews under Islam* (London: I. B. Tauris, 1996), 61.
2 Abdel-Raouf Sinno, *Deutsche Interessen in Syrien und Palästina 1841–1898* (Berlin: Baalbek Verlag, 1982), 11.

3 A. L. Tibawi, *British Interests in Palestine 1800–1901* (Oxford: Oxford University Press, 1961), 16.
4 Roderic H. Davison, *Reform in the Ottoman Empire, 1856–1876*, repr. ed. (Princeton, N.J.: Princeton University Press, 2016).

2 RELIGIOUS MOBILITY

1 Salim Daccache, "Catholic Missions in the Middle East," in *Christianity: A History in the Middle East*, ed. Habib Badr (Beirut: World Council of Churches, 2005), 694.
2 Daccache, "Catholic Missions in the Middle East," 696.
3 John Hubers, *I Am a Pilgrim, a Traveler, a Stranger: Exploring the Life and Mind of the First American Missionary to the Middle East, the Rev. Pliny Fisk* (Eugene, Ore.: Pickwick, 2016), 116.
4 Mitri Raheb, *Das reformatorische Erbe unter den Palästinensern: Zur Entstehung der Evangelisch-Lutherischen Kirche in Jordanien*, vol. 11, Reihe: Die Lutherische Kirche. Geschichte und Gestalten (Gütersloh: Gütersloher Verlagshaus, Gerd Mohn, 1990), 24.
5 Peter Kawerau, *Amerika und die orientalischen Kirchen: Ursprung und Anfang der amerikanischen Mission unter den Nationalkirchen Westasiens*, Arbeiten Zur Kirchengeschichte 31 (Bethlehem: Diyar, 2017), 171.
6 Tibawi, *British Interests in Palestine 1800–1901*, 12.
7 Sinno, *Deutsche Interessen in Syrien und Palästina 1841–1898*, 19.
8 Sinno, *Deutsche Interessen in Syrien und Palästina 1841–1898*, 79.
9 Raheb, *Das reformatorische Erbe unter den Palästinensern*, 105.
10 Tibawi, *British Interests in Palestine 1800–1901*, 84.
11 Raheb, *Das reformatorische Erbe unter den Palästinensern*, 42–58.
12 For further reading, see Ḥabīb Badr, "Mission to 'Nominal Christians': The Policy and Practice of American Board of Commissioners for Foreign Missions and Its Missionaries Concerning Eastern Churches Which Led to the Organization of a Protestant Church in Beirut (1819–1848)" (PhD diss., Princeton Theological Seminary, Princeton, N.J., 1992).
13 Heather J. Sharkey, *American Evangelicals in Egypt: Missionary Encounters in an Age of Empire*, repr. ed. (Princeton, N.J.: Princeton University Press, 2015).
14 Edward W. Said, *Orientalism* (New York: Vintage, 1979).
15 Sharkey, *American Evangelicals in Egypt*, 19.

16 For the full story of As'ad Shidyaq, see Ussama Makdisi, *Artillery of Heaven: American Missionaries and the Failed Conversion of the Middle East* (Ithaca, N.Y.: Cornell University Press, 2009).
17 Makdisi, *Artillery of Heaven*, 113.
18 Makdisi, *Artillery of Heaven*, 125.
19 Daccache, "Catholic Missions in the Middle East," 699.
20 Daccache, "Catholic Missions in the Middle East," 700.
21 Daccache, "Catholic Missions in the Middle East," 701.
22 Hanna Kildani, *Modern Christianity in the Holy Land* (Bloomington, Ind.: AuthorHouse, 2010), 244–90.
23 Daccache, "Catholic Missions in the Middle East," 704.
24 Sharkey, *American Evangelicals in Egypt*, 47.
25 Derek Hopwood, *The Russian Presence in Syria & Palestine 1843–1914* (Oxford: Clarendon, 1969).

3   A MASSACRE ON MOUNT LEBANON

1 Courbage and Fargues, *Christians and Jews under Islam*, 99–109.
2 Bruce Masters, *Christians and Jews in the Ottoman Arab World: The Roots of Sectarianism*, rev. ed. (Cambridge: Cambridge University Press, 2004), 156–65.
3 Makdisi, *Culture of Sectarianism*, 29.
4 Makdisi, *Culture of Sectarianism*, 8.
5 Makdisi, *Culture of Sectarianism*, 60.
6 Makdisi, *Culture of Sectarianism*, 68.
7 Makdisi, *Culture of Sectarianism*, 80.
8 Makdisi, *Culture of Sectarianism*, 68.
9 Augustus Johnson, "The Massacre in Syria: Letter from the American Consul at Beirut," *New York Times*, August 10, 1860, https://www.nytimes.com/1860/08/10/archives/the-massacre-in-syria-letter-from-the-american-consul-at-beirut.html.
10 Charles Henry Churchill, *The Druzes and the Maronites under the Turkish Rule, from 1840 to 1860* (London: Bernard Quaritch, 1862), 177.
11 Churchill, *Druzes and the Maronites under the Turkish Rule*, 189–90.
12 Makdisi, *Culture of Sectarianism*, 169.
13 Jens Hanssen, Hicham Safieddine, and Ussama Samir Makdisi, *The Clarion of Syria: A Patriot's Call against the Civil War of 1860* (Oakland: University of California Press, 2019), 84.
14 Hanssen, Safieddine, and Makdisi, *Clarion of Syria*, 81.
15 Hanssen, Safieddine, and Makdisi, *Clarion of Syria*, 82.

16 Hanssen, Safieddine, and Makdisi, *Clarion of Syria*, 82.
17 Hanssen, Safieddine, and Makdisi, *Clarion of Syria*, 99.
18 Hanssen, Safieddine, and Makdisi, *Clarion of Syria*, 78.
19 Hanssen, Safieddine, and Makdisi, *Clarion of Syria*, 111.
20 Hanssen, Safieddine, and Makdisi, *Clarion of Syria*, 72.
21 Hanssen, Safieddine, and Makdisi, *Clarion of Syria*, 67.
22 Hanssen, Safieddine, and Makdisi, *Clarion of Syria*, 117.
23 Hanssen, Safieddine, and Makdisi, *Clarion of Syria*, 77.
24 Hanssen, Safieddine, and Makdisi, *Clarion of Syria*, 54.
25 Hanssen, Safieddine, and Makdisi, *Clarion of Syria*, 109.
26 Hanssen, Safieddine, and Makdisi, *Clarion of Syria*, 74.
27 Hanssen, Safieddine, and Makdisi, *Clarion of Syria*, 31.

4 AGENTS OF RENAISSANCE

1 Leila Tarazi Fawaz, *Merchants and Migrants in Nineteenth-Century Beirut* (Cambridge, Mass.: Harvard University Press, 2000), 44–60.
2 Michael J. Reimer, *Colonial Bridgehead: Government and Society in Alexandria, 1807–1882*, repr. ed. (London: Routledge, 2019), 90–110.
3 Mark Levine, *Overthrowing Geography: Jaffa, Tel Aviv, and the Struggle for Palestine, 1880–1948* (Berkeley: University of California Press, 2005), 15–28.
4 A. Adnan Musallam, "The Formative Stages of Palestinian Arab Immigration to Latin America and Immigrants' Quest for Return and for the Palestinian Citizenship in the Early 1920's," in *Latin American with Palestinian Roots*, ed. Viola Raheb (Bethlehem: Diyar, 2012), 17.
5 Alixa Naff, *Becoming American: The Early Arab Immigrant Experience*, M.E.R.I. Special Studies (Carbondale: Southern Illinois University Press, 1993), 110.
6 Dalia Abdelhady, *The Lebanese Diaspora: The Arab Immigrant Experience in Montreal, New York, and Paris* (New York: New York University Press, 2011), 6.
7 Viola Raheb, "Sisters and Brothers in the Diaspora: Palestinian Christians in Latin America," in Raheb, *Latin American with Palestinian Roots*, 9.
8 Ilan Pappé, *The Modern Middle East: A Social and Cultural History*, 3rd ed. (New York: Routledge, 2014), 198–203.

9 Eleanor Tejirian and Reeva Spector Simon, *Conflict, Conquest, and Conversion: Two Thousand Years of Christian Missions in the Middle East*, repr. ed. (New York: Columbia University Press, 2014), 101–2.

10 Masters, *Christians and Jews in the Ottoman Arab World*, 151.

11 Raheb, *Das reformatorische Erbe unter den Palästinensern*, 62–77.

12 Tejirian and Simon, *Conflict, Conquest, and Conversion*, 189.

13 Samir Khalaf, *Protestant Missionaries in the Levant: Ungodly Puritans, 1820–1860* (New York: Routledge, 2017), 214–51.

14 Fruma Zachs, "Feminism for Men: A Note on Butrus al-Bustani's *Lecture on the Education of Women* (1849)," in *Butrus al-Bustani: Spirit of the Age*, ed. Adel Beshara (Melbourne: Iphoenix, 2014), 113–30, https://www.academia.edu/15885629/Feminism_for_Men_A_Note_on_Butrus_al-Bustanis_Lecture_on_the_Education_of_Women_1849_.

15 Ela Greenberg, *Preparing the Mothers of Tomorrow: Education and Islam in Mandate Palestine* (Austin: University of Texas Press, 2010), 3.

16 Sharkey, *American Evangelicals in Egypt*, 42.

17 Hopwood, *Russian Presence in Syria & Palestine 1843–1914*, 37–41.

5 CHRISTIAN ZIONISM

1 Courbage and Fargues, *Christians and Jews under Islam*, 81–83.

2 Robert O. Smith, *More Desired Than Our Owne Salvation: The Roots of Christian Zionism* (New York: Oxford University Press, 2013), 114.

3 For more on Lord Shaftesbury, see Donald M. Lewis, *The Origins of Christian Zionism: Lord Shaftesbury and Evangelical Support for a Jewish Homeland*, repr. ed. (New York: Cambridge University Press, 2014).

4 Nur Masalha, *The Zionist Bible: Biblical Precedent, Colonialism and the Erasure of Memory* (New York: Routledge, 2014), 83.

5 Lucien Wolf, *Notes on the Diplomatic History of the Jewish Question: With Texts of Protocols, Treaty Stipulations and Other Public Acts and Official Documents* (London: Spottiswoode, 1919), 119, http://archive.org/details/notesondiplomati00wolfuoft.

6 Wolf, *Notes on the Diplomatic History of the Jewish Question*, 120.

7 Shlomo Sand, *The Invention of the Jewish People*, trans. Yael Lotan (London: Verso, 2010).

8 Wolf, *Notes on the Diplomatic History of the Jewish Question*, 121.

9 Two good sources on Christian Zionism are Goran Gunner and Robert O. Smith, eds., *Comprehending Christian Zionism: Perspectives in Comparison* (Minneapolis: Fortress, 2014); and Stephen Sizer and David G. Peterson, *Christian Zionism: Road-Map to Armageddon?* IVP/UK ed. (Leicester: IVP Academic, 2006).

10 Edwin Hodder, *The Life and Work of the Seventh Earl of Shaftesbury, K.G.*, vol. 2 (London: Cassell, 1886), 14.

11 Theodor Herzl, *The Jewish State: An Attempt at a Modern Solution of the Jewish Question*, ed. Jacob Haas, trans. Sylvie d'Avigdor, repr. ed. (Whithorn, UK: Anodos Books, 2018).

12 Khalidi, *Hundred Years' War on Palestine*, 17–54.

13 Jacob Norris, *Land of Progress: Palestine in the Age of Colonial Development, 1905–1948* (Oxford: Oxford University Press, 2013), 8.

14 Smith, *More Desired Than Our Owne Salvation*, 185.

6 THE ROAD TO GENOCIDE

1 Frederick F. Anscombe, *State, Faith, and Nation in Ottoman and Post-Ottoman Lands* (New York: Cambridge University Press, 2014), 61–89.

2 Negib Azoury, *Le reveil de la nation arabe*, repr. ed. (Whitefish, Mont.: Kessinger, 2010).

3 The latest summary of the research on this issue is found in Lucien J. Frary and Mara Kozelsky, eds., *Russian-Ottoman Borderlands: The Eastern Question Reconsidered* (Madison: University of Wisconsin Press, 2014).

4 Ronald Grigor Suny, Fatma Muge Gocek, and Norman M. Naimark, eds., *A Question of Genocide: Armenians and Turks at the End of the Ottoman Empire* (Oxford: Oxford University Press, 2011).

5 Erik Jan Zurcher, "Young Turks, Ottoman Muslims and Turkish Nationalist Identity Politics 1908–1938," in *Ottoman Past and Today's Turkey*, ed. K. H. Karpat (Leiden: Brill, 2000), https://www.academia.edu/5726070/Young_Turks_Ottoman_Muslims_and_Turkish_Nationalists_Identity_Politics_1908-1938.

6 Exact numbers are not available. To the different estimates, see Courbage and Fargues, *Christians and Jews under Islam*, 109–15.

7 Courbage and Fargues, *Christians and Jews under Islam*, 109–15.

8 Courbage and Fargues, *Christians and Jews under Islam*, 123–29.

9 An excellent overview of the recent scholarship on the Armenian Genocide is Bedross Der Matossian, "'Explaining the Unexplainable: Recent Trends in the Armenian Genocide Historiography,"

Journal of Levantine Studies 5, no. 2 (2015): 143–66, https://www
.academia.edu/26383605/Bedross_Der_Matossian_Explaining
_the_Unexplainable_Recent_Trends_in_the_Armenian
_Genocide_Historiography_in_Journal_of_Levantine_Studies
_Vol_5_No_2_Winter_2015_pp_143_166.

10 Vahakn N. Dadrian, *The History of the Armenian Genocide: Ethnic
Conflict from the Balkans to Anatolia to the Caucasus* (New York:
Berghahn Books, 2003).

11 Stephen R. Graubard and Richard G. Hovannisian, eds., *The Armenian Genocide in Perspective* (Abingdon; New York: Routledge, 2017).

12 Suny, Gocek, and Naimark, *Question of Genocide.*

13 Vahakn N. Dadrian, *German Responsibility in the Armenian Genocide: A Review of the Historical Evidence of German Complicity,* 3rd
ed. (Watertown, Mass.: Blue Crane Books, 1996).

14 Wolfgang Gust, *The Armenian Genocide: Evidence from the German
Foreign Office Archives, 1915–1916* (New York: Berghahn Books,
2013), 68.

15 Dadrian, *German Responsibility in the Armenian Genocide,* 22, nn.
37–42.

16 Gust, *Armenian Genocide,* 68, n. 280.

17 Dadrian, *German Responsibility in the Armenian Genocide,* 19.

18 Gust, *Armenian Genocide,* 158, n. 181.

19 Dadrian, *German Responsibility in the Armenian Genocide,* 156, n. 178.

20 Dadrian, *German Responsibility in the Armenian Genocide,* 156, n. 177.

21 Dadrian, *German Responsibility in the Armenian Genocide,* 126, n. 143.

22 Gust, *Armenian Genocide,* 89, n. 407.

7 MINORITIES IN NATION-STATES

1 Mitri Raheb, "Palestinian Christians in Modern History: Between
Migration and Displacement," in *Palestinian Christians: Emigra-
tion, Displacement and Diaspora,* ed. Mitri Raheb (Bethlehem:
Diyar, 2017), 11.

2 Abdelhady, *Lebanese Diaspora,* 6.

3 William Harris, *Lebanon: A History, 600–2011,* repr. ed. (Oxford:
Oxford University Press, 2014), 147–92.

4 Johnny Mansour, *A New Vision of the Life and Works of Bishop Gregorios Hajjar,* new ed. (Haifa: Al-Hakeem 2013).

5 For a detailed account on the Assyrians in Iraq, see Sargon Donabed,
*Reforging a Forgotten History: Iraq and the Assyrians in the Twentieth
Century,* repr. ed. (Edinburgh: Edinburgh University Press, 2016).

6   Robson, *States of Separation*.

7   Laura Robson, *Colonialism and Christianity in Mandate Palestine*, repr. ed. (Austin: University of Texas Press, 2012), 158.

8   Benjamin Thomas White, *The Emergence of Minorities in the Middle East: The Politics of Community in French Mandate Syria*, repr. ed. (Edinburgh: Edinburgh University Press, 2012).

9   Robson, *Minorities and the Modern Arab World*.

10 Konstantinos Papastathis and Ruth Kark, "Colonialism and Religious Power Politics: The Question of New Regulations within the Orthodox Church of Jerusalem during the British Mandate," *Middle Eastern Studies* 50, no. 4 (2014): 589–605.

11 Raheb, *Das reformatorische Erbe unter den Palästinensern*, 135–50.

12 Sharkey, *American Evangelicals in Egypt*, 149–78.

13 Pappé, *Modern Middle East*, 138–41.

14 Carlotta Stegagno, "The Foundation of the Ba'th Party: The Ideology of Michel 'Aflaq," https://www.academia.edu/16561697/The _foundation_of_the_Bath_Party_the_ideology_of_Michel_Aflaq.

15 For further reading, see Salim Mujais, *The Syrian Social Nationalist Party: Its Ideology and History* (London: Black House, 2019).

16 Martyn Frampton, *The Muslim Brotherhood and the West: A History of Enmity and Engagement* (Cambridge, Mass.: Belknap Press, 2018), 11–57.

17 Robson, *Minorities and the Modern Arab World*.

8   A CATASTROPHE

1   Raheb, "Palestinian Christians in Modern History," 12.

2   Musallam, "Formative Stages of Palestinian Arab Immigration to Latin America," 15–24.

3   Raheb, "Palestinian Christians in Modern History," 13.

4   Johnny Mansour, *Arab Christians in Israel: Facts, Figures and Trends* (Bethlehem: Diyar, 2012), 15.

5   "Iqrit Heritage Society," accessed December 18, 2020, iqrit.org/ eng/chron.htm.

6   Benny Morris, "Operation Hiram Revisited: A Correction," *Journal of Palestine Studies* 28, no. 2 (1999): 68–76.

7   For more on the definition, methodology, and execution of ethnic cleansing in Palestine, see Pappé, *Ethnic Cleansing of Palestine*.

8   "Iqrit Heritage Society."

9   Geremy Forman and Alexandre (Sandy) Kedar, "From Arab Land to 'Israel Lands': The Legal Dispossession of the Palestinians Dis-

placed by Israel in the Wake of 1948," *Environment and Planning D: Society and Space* 22, no. 6 (2004): 809–30.

10 Seth J. Frantzman and Ruth Kark, "The Catholic Church in Palestine/Israel: Real Estate in Terra Sancta," *Middle Eastern Studies* 50, no. 3 (2014): 370–96, https://doi.org/10.1068/d402.

11 Seth J. Frantzman, Benjamin W. Glueckstadt, and Ruth Kark, "The Anglican Church in Palestine and Israel: Colonialism, Arabization and Land Ownership," *Middle Eastern Studies* 47, no. 1 (2011): 101–26, https://doi.org/10.1080/00263201003590482.

12 Itamar Katz and Ruth Kark, "The Church and Landed Property: The Greek Orthodox Patriarchate of Jerusalem," *Middle Eastern Studies* 43, no. 3 (2007): 383–408, https://doi.org/10.1080/00263200701245969.

13 Raheb, *Das reformatorische Erbe unter den Palästinensern*, 191–93.

14 Raheb, *Das reformatorische Erbe unter den Palästinensern*, 201–5.

15 Lutheran World Federation, "Jerusalem Program," accessed June 13, 2020, https://jerusalem.lutheranworld.org.

16 DSPR | Middle East Council of Churches, Department of Service to Palestinian Refugees, accessed June 13, 2020, https://dsprme.org/.

17 CNEWA | Catholic Near East Welfare Association, accessed June 13, 2020, https://cnewa.org/.

18 It was this same church that used the Bible in a similar way to colonize South Africa and to legitimize the apartheid system.

19 Walter Kickel, *Das gelobte Land: Die religiöse Bedeutung des Staates Israel in jüdischer und christlicher Sicht* (Munich: Kösel, 1984), 158–66.

20 For further reading, see Arthur Allen Cohen, *The Myth of the Judeo-Christian Tradition, and Other Dissenting Essays* (New York: Schocken Books, 1971).

21 Noura Erakat, "Whiteness as Property in Israel: Revival, Rehabilitation, and Removal," *Harvard Journal of Ethnic and Racial Justice* 69 (2015): 69–104, https://www.academia.edu/33926126/Whiteness_as_Property_in_Israel_Revival_Rehabilitation_and_Removal.

9   ARAB AND CHRISTIAN

1 NESSL | National Evangelical Synod of Syria and Lebanon, accessed November 10, 2020, http://synod-sl.org/.

2 National Evangelical Church of Beirut, accessed November 10, 2020, http://forum.nechurchbeirut.com/.

3 Raheb, *Das reformatorische Erbe unter den Palästinensern*, 213–19.

4   Episcopal Diocese of Jerusalem, accessed November 10, 2020, https://www.j-diocese.org/.

5   Sharkey, *American Evangelicals in Egypt*, 191–210.

6   Middle East Council of Churches, accessed November 10, 2020, https://www.mecc.org/.

7   Pappé, *Modern Middle East*, 154–57.

8   S. S. Hasan, *Christians versus Muslims in Modern Egypt: The Century-Long Struggle for Coptic Equality* (Oxford: Oxford University Press, 2003), 57–101.

9   Pappé, *Modern Middle East*, 157.

10 Pappé, *Modern Middle East*, 142–44.

10   A TURNING POINT

1   Avi Sagi and Dov Schwartz, *Religious Zionism and the Six Day War: From Realism to Messianism* (London: Routledge, 2018), 76–109.

2   David S. New, *Holy War: The Rise of Militant Christian, Jewish and Islamic Fundamentalism* (Jefferson, N.C.: McFarland, 2001), 155.

3   New, *Holy War*, 154.

4   Hal Lindsey and Carole C. Carlson, *The Late Great Planet Earth* (Grand Rapids: Zondervan Academic, 1970).

5   Stephen R. Haynes, "Christian Holocaust Theology: A Critical Reassessment," *Journal of the American Academy of Religion* 62, no. 2 (1994): 553–85.

6   Khalidi, *Hundred Years' War on Palestine*, 96–138.

7   Mitri Raheb and Suzanne Watts Henderson, *The Cross in Contexts: Suffering and Redemption in Palestine* (Maryknoll, N.Y.: Orbis, 2017), 73–92.

8   Mitri Raheb, "Displacement Theopolitics," in *The Invention of History: A Century of Interplay between Theology and Politics in Palestine*, ed. Mitri Raheb (Bethlehem: Diyar, 2011), 23–24.

9   Nelly van Doorn-Harder, ed., *Between Desert and City: The Coptic Orthodox Church Today*, repr. ed. (Eugene, Ore.: Wipf & Stock, 2012).

10 Nelly van Doorn-Harder, "Kyrillos VI (1902–1971): Planner, Patriarch and Saint," in Doorn-Harder, *Between Desert and City*, 231–43.

11 Nelly van Doorn-Harder, "Signposts to Biography: Pope Shenouda III," in Doorn-Harder, *Between Desert and City*, 244–54.

12 Alexander D. M. Henley, "Politics of a Church at War: Maronite Catholicism in the Lebanese Civil War," *Mediterranean Politics* 13, no. 3 (2008): 353–69.

13 Fiona McCallum, John Anderson, and Raymond Hinnebusch, *Christian Religious Leadership in the Middle East: The Political Role of Patriarch* (Lewiston, N.Y.: Edwin Mellen, 2010), 159–90.

11 PETRODOLLARS

1 Mitri Raheb, "Christianity in the Middle East, 1917–2017," in *History of Global Christianity*, vol. 3, ed. Jens Holger Schjørring, Norman Hjelm, and Kevin Ward (Boston: Brill, 2018), 389.

2 David Commins, *The Wahhabi Mission and Saudi Arabia* (London: I. B. Tauris, 2006).

3 François de Bel-Air, "Migration Profile," Migration Policy Centre Policy Briefs, 2017/12, https://www.academia.edu/33464564/Migration_Profile_Lebanon.

4 Paul Tabar, "Lebanon: A Country of Emigration and Immigration," 5, accessed July 4, 2020, https://www.academia.edu/31369352/Lebanon_A_Country_of_Emigration_and_Immigration.

5 Anthony Arnove, ed., *Iraq under Siege, Updated Edition: The Deadly Impact of Sanctions and War*, rev. ed. (Cambridge, Mass.: South End Press, 2003).

6 Géraldine Chatelard, "Migration from Iraq between the Gulf and the Iraq Wars (1990–2003): Historical and Sociospacial Dimensions" (Centre on Migration, Policy and Society, 2009), https://www.academia.edu/182775/Migration_from_Iraq_between_the_Gulf_and_the_Iraq_Wars_1990-2003_Historical_and_Sociospacial_Dimensions.

7 For further reading, see Jok Moduk Jok, *Sudan: Race, Religion, and Violence* (Oxford: Oneworld, 2015).

8 Abdel Monem Said Aly and Manfred W. Wenner, "Modern Islamic Reform Movements: The Muslim Brotherhood in Contemporary Egypt," *Middle East Journal* 36, no. 3 (1982): 336–61.

9 Nathan J. Brown and Amr Hamzawy, *Between Religion and Politics* (Washington, D.C.: Carnegie Endowment for International Peace, 2010), 9–46.

10 Raphael Lefevre, *Ashes of Hama: The Muslim Brotherhood in Syria* (New York: Oxford University Press, 2013), 115–21.

11 Lawrence Rubin, "Politics, Religion and Ideology: The Rise of Official Islam in Jordan," *Politics, Religion & Ideology* 14, no. 1 (2013): 59–74, https://www.academia.edu/23847994/Politics_Religion_and_Ideology_The_Rise_of_Official_Islam_in_Jordan.

12 Brown and Hamzawy, *Between Religion and Politics*, 161–80.

13 Frederic Wehrey, *Sectarian Politics in the Gulf: From the Iraq War to the Arab Uprisings*, repr. ed. (New York: Columbia University Press, 2016), 207–19.

14 Yvonne Haddad and Rahel Fischbach, "Interfaith Dialogue in Lebanon: Between a Power Balancing Act and Theological Encounters," *Islam and Christian Muslim Relations* 26, no. 4 (2015): 429–30, https://www.academia.edu/17740013/Interfaith_Dialogue_in_Lebanon.

15 IEIC | Université Saint-Joseph de Beyrouth, Institut d'études Islamo-Chrétiennes, accessed November 11, 2020, https://www.usj.edu.lb/ieic/.

16 University of Balamand, accessed July 19, 2020, http://www.balamand.edu.lb/home/Pages/default.aspx.

17 AGMCD | Arab Group for Muslim-Christian Dialogue, accessed November 11, 2020, http://www.agmcd.org/.

18 Al-Liqa' Center, accessed November 11, 2020, http://al-liqacenter.org.ps/eng/.

19 Sabeel Ecumenical Liberation Theology Center, accessed November 11, 2020, https://sabeel.org/.

20 Diyar | Diyar Consortium, accessed November 11, 2020, https://www.diyar.ps/en.

21 The Holy Land Ecumenical Foundation has recognized the conciliatory achievements of Patriarch Shabbah with a collection of his essays (Michel Shabbah, *Faithful Witness: On Reconciliation and Peace in the Holy Land* [New York: New City Press, 2008]). See https://hcef.org/97-drew-christiansen-and-saliba-sarsar-qmichel-sabbah-faithful-witness/.

22 Kairos Palestine, accessed July 19, 2020, https://kairospalestine.ps/.

23 Peter E. Makari, *Conflict and Cooperation: Christian-Muslim Relations in Contemporary Egypt* (Syracuse, N.Y.: Syracuse University Press, 2007), 159.

24 Edith Szanto, "Inter-religious Dialogue in Syria: Politics, Ethics and Miscommunication," *Political Theology* 9, no. 1 (2008): 94.

25 Royal Institute for Inter-faith Studies, accessed November 11, 2020, http://www.riifs.org/en/home.

26 The Amman Message, accessed November 11, 2020, http://ammanmessage.com/.

27 A Common Word, accessed November 11, 2020, https://www.acommonword.com/introduction-to-a-common-word-between-us-and-you/.

28 DICID | Doha International Center for Interfaith Dialogue, accessed November 11, 2020, http://www.dicid.org/.

29 "Document on Human Fraternity for World Peace and Living Together," *Vatican News*, February 4, 2019, https://www.vaticannews.va/en/pope/news/2019-02/pope-francis-uae-declaration-with-al-azhar-grand-imam.html.

30 John J. Mearsheimer and Stephen M. Walt, *The Israel Lobby and U.S. Foreign Policy* (New York: FSG Adult, 2008).

31 Razek Siriani, "Syria," in *Christianity in North Africa and West Asia*, ed. Kenneth R. Ross, Mariz Tadros, and Todd M. Johnson (Edinburgh: Edinburgh University Press, 2018), 108.

12 CHALLENGING TIMES

1 Christian Academic Forum for Citizenship, accessed November 11, 2020, http://cafcaw.org/.

2 Marina Eleftheriadou, "Christian Militias in Syria and Iraq: Beyond the Neutrality/Passivity Debate," *Middle East Bulletin* 28 (2015): 13–19, https://www.academia.edu/13467603/Christian_militias_in_Syria_and_Iraq_beyond_the_neutrality_passivity_debate.

3 World Bank, "Data: Middle East and North Africa," accessed November 11, 2020, https://data.worldbank.org/region/middle-east-and-north-africa.

4 Arab Human Development Report, *Youth and the Prospect for Human Development in a Changing Reality*, 2016, 32, https://arab-hdr.org/report/youth-2016/.

5 Eleftheriadou, "Christian Militias in Syria and Iraq."

6 Arab Human Development Report, *Youth and the Prospect for Human Development*.

7 United Nations Development Programme, *Human Development Reports*, accessed February 12, 2021, http://www.hdr.undp.org/en/content/human-development-report-1994.

8 *From the Nile to the Euphrates: The Call of Faith and Citizenship* (Bethlehem: Diyar, 2015), 9–10.

9   "Military Spending in MENA by Selected Country 2019," *Statista*, 2020, https://www.statista.com/statistics/676109/mena-military -spending-by-selected-country/.

10 "Egypt Fourth Highest Illiteracy Rate in Arab World," *Middle East Monitor*, September 8, 2016, https://www.middleeastmonitor .com/20160908-egypt-fourth-highest-illiteracy-rate-in-arab -world/.

11 Facundo Alvaredo and Thomas Piketty, "Measuring Top Incomes and Inequality in the Middle East: Data Limitations and Illustra- tion with the Case of Egypt," April 13, 2014, http://piketty.pse.ens .fr/files/AlvaredoPiketty2014MiddleEast.pdf.

12 *From the Nile to the Euphrates*, 10–11.

13 Jonathan Fox, *A World Survey of Religion and the State* (Cambridge: Cambridge University Press, 2008), 218–48.

14 Raoul Wootliff, "Final Text of Jewish Nation-State Law, Approved by the Knesset Early on July 19," *Times of Israel*, July 19, 2018, https://www.timesofisrael.com/final-text-of-jewish-nation-state -bill-set-to-become-law/.

15 Pew Forum on Religion and Public Life, accessed November 11, 2020, https://www.pewforum.org/.

16 United Nations, Universal Declaration of Human Rights, accessed November 11, 2020, https://www.un.org/en/universal-declaration -human-rights/index.html.

17 Office of the High Commissioner for Human Rights (UN Human Rights), International Covenant on Civil and Political Rights, accessed November 11, 2020, https://www.ohchr.org/EN/ProfessionalInterest/ Pages/CCPR.aspx.

18 Arab Human Development Report, *Youth and the Prospect for Human Development*, 7.

19 Bessma Momani, *Arab Dawn: Arab Youth and the Demographic Divi- dend They Will Bring* (Toronto: University of Toronto Press, 2015), 27.

20 Momani, *Arab Dawn*, 36–37.

21 Momani, *Arab Dawn*, 11.

22 Richard Florida | Creative Class Group, accessed November 11, 2020, http://www.creativeclass.com/richard_florida.

23 For more on the theory of "relative deprivation," see Ted Robert Gurr, *Why Men Rebel* (New York: Routledge, 2011).

24 Mitri Raheb, ed., *Middle Eastern Women: The Intersection of Law, Culture and Religion* (Bethlehem: Diyar, 2020).

25 Office of the High Commissioner for Human Rights (UN Human Rights), Convention on the Elimination of All Forms of Discrimination against Women, accessed November 11, 2020, https://www.ohchr.org/EN/ProfessionalInterest/Pages/CEDAW.aspx.

26 Max-Planck-Gesellschaft, "Climate-Exodus Expected in the Middle East and North Africa," accessed November 11, 2020, https://www.mpg.de/10481936/climate-change-middle-east-north-africa.

27 Jeremy S. Pal and Elfatih A. B. Eltahir, "Future Temperature in Southwest Asia Projected to Exceed a Threshold for Human Adaptability," *Nature Climate Change* 6, no. 2 (2016): 197–200, https://doi.org/10.1038/nclimate2833.

28 Max-Planck-Gesellschaft, "Climate-Exodus Expected in the Middle East and North Africa."

29 United Nations, Universal Declaration of Human Rights.

EPILOGUE

1 See, for instance, Luis Bush, "The Challenge before Us," in *Proclaim Christ until He Comes: Calling the Whole Church to Take the Whole Gospel to the Whole World*, ed. J. D. Douglas (Minneapolis: World Wide, 1990), 61, https://web.archive.org/web/20110610230732/http://www.lausanne.org/documents/lau2docs/058.pdf.

2 Melani McAlister, "The Politics of Persecution," *Middle East Report* 249 (2008), 20, https://merip.org/2008/12/the-politics-of-persecution/.

3 McAlister, "Politics of Persecution," 22–24.

4 International Religious Freedom Act of 1998, H.R. 2431, 105th Congress (1998), https://www.congress.gov/bill/105th-congress/house-bill/2431.

5 The mandate for this position recently received renewal; see ADF International, "European Commission Revives Special Envoy on Freedom of Religion or Belief," July 9, 2020, https://adfinternational.org/news/european-commission-revives-special-envoy-on-freedom-of-religion-or-belief/.

6 McAlister, "Politics of Persecution," 20.

7 Michael Pence, "Remarks by Vice President Pence at the World Summit in Defense of Persecuted Christians," May 11, 2017,

https://trumpwhitehouse.archives.gov/briefings-statements/
remarks-vice-president-pence-world-summit-defense-persecuted
-christians/.

8   In Defense of Christians, accessed November 11, 2020, http://
indefenseofchristians.org/.

9   Michael Pence, "Remarks by the Vice President at In Defense of
Christians Solidarity Dinner," White House, October 25, 2017,
https://trumpwhitehouse.archives.gov/briefings-statements/
remarks-vice-president-defense-christians-solidarity-dinner/.

10 United States Department of State, Declaration of Principles for the
International Religious Freedom Alliance, February 5, 2020, https://
www.state.gov/declaration-of-principles-for-the-international
-religious-freedom-alliance/.

11 Mahmoud Darwish, *Unfortunately, It Was Paradise: Selected Poems*,
trans. and ed. Sinan Antoon and Carolyn Forché (Berkeley: University of California Press, 2003, 2013), 21.

12 *From the Nile to the Euphrates*, 17–18.

BIBLIOGRAPHY

OFFICIAL DOCUMENTS AND REPORTS

The Amman Message. Accessed November 11, 2020. http://ammanmessage.com/.

Arab Human Development Report. *Youth and the Prospect for Human Development in a Changing Reality.* 2016. https://arab-hdr.org/report/youth-2016/.

Bel-Air, Françoise de. "Migration Profile: Lebanon." Migration Policy Centre Policy Briefs, 2017/12. https://www.academia.edu/33464564/Migration_Profile_Lebanon.

A Common Word. Accessed November 11, 2020. https://www.acommonword.com/introduction-to-a-common-word-between-us-and-you/.

"Document on Human Fraternity for World Peace and Living Together." *Vatican News*, February 4, 2019. https://www.vaticannews.va/en/pope/news/2019-02/pope-francis-uae-declaration-with-al-azhar-grand-imam.html.

International Religious Freedom Act of 1998, H.R.2431, 105th Congress (1998). https://www.congress.gov/bill/105th-congress/house-bill/2431.

Max-Planck-Gesellschaft. "Climate-Exodus Expected in the Middle East and North Africa." Accessed November 11, 2020. https://www.mpg.de/10481936/climate-change-middle-east-north-africa.

"Military Spending in MENA by Selected Country 2019." *Statista*, 2019. https://www.statista.com/statistics/676109/mena-military-spending-by-selected-country/.

Office of the High Commissioner for Human Rights (UN Human Rights). Convention on the Elimination of All Forms of

Discrimination against Women. Accessed July 19, 2020. https://www.ohchr.org/EN/ProfessionalInterest/Pages/CEDAW.aspx.

Office of the High Commissioner for Human Rights (UN Human Rights). International Covenant on Civil and Political Rights. Accessed November 11, 2020. https://www.ohchr.org/EN/ProfessionalInterest/Pages/CCPR.aspx.

Pence, Mike. "Remarks by the Vice President at In Defense of Christians Solidarity Dinner." White House, October 25, 2017. https://trumpwhitehouse.archives.gov/briefings-statements/remarks-vice-president-defense-christians-solidarity-dinner/.

———. "Remarks by Vice President Pence at the World Summit in Defense of Persecuted Christians." White House, May 11, 2017. https://trumpwhitehouse.archives.gov/briefings-statements/remarks-vice-president-pence-world-summit-defense-persecuted-christians/.

Pew Forum on Religion and Public Life. "How Religious Restrictions Have Risen around the World." July 15, 2019. https://www.pewforum.org/2019/07/15/a-closer-look-at-how-religious-restrictions-have-risen-around-the-world/.

United Nations. Universal Declaration of Human Rights. Accessed November 11, 2020. https://www.un.org/en/universal-declaration-human-rights/index.html.

United States Department of State. Declaration of Principles for the International Religious Freedom Alliance. February 5, 2020. https://www.state.gov/declaration-of-principles-for-the-international-religious-freedom-alliance/.

United States Commission on International Religious Freedom. "Countries of Particular Concern." Accessed June 22, 2021. https://www.uscirf.gov/countries/.

The World Bank. "Climate Change in the Middle East & North Africa." Accessed November 12, 2020. https://www.worldbank.org/en/programs/mena-climate-change.

———. "Data: Middle East and North Africa." Accessed November 11, 2020. https://data.worldbank.org/region/middle-east-and-north-africa.

NEWS ARTICLES

ADF International. "European Commission Revives Special Envoy on Freedom of Religion or Belief." July 9, 2020. https://adfinternational.org/news/european-commission-revives-special-envoy-on-freedom-of-religion-or-belief/.

Dias, Elizabeth. "Ted Cruz Was Booed Off Stage at Christian Event." *Time*, September 11, 2014. https://time.com/3328063/ted-cruz-booed-israel-christian-middle-east/.

"Egypt Fourth Highest Illiteracy Rate in Arab World." *Middle East Monitor*, September 8, 2016. Accessed November 11, 2020. https://www.middleeastmonitor.com/20160908-egypt-fourth-highest-illiteracy-rate-in-arab-world/.

Johnson, Augustus. "The Massacre in Syria: Letter from the American Consul at Beirut." *New York Times*, August 10, 1860. https://www.nytimes.com/1860/08/10/archives/the-massacre-in-syria-letter-from-the-american-consul-at-beirut.html.

Strode, Tom. "Christian Persecution Focus of Global Summit." Baptist Press, May 12, 2017. http://www.bpnews.net/48862/christian-persecution-focus-of-global-summit.

Toosi, Nahhal, and Gabby Orr. "Trump Weighs Conditioning Foreign Aid on Religious Freedom." *Politico*, November 12, 2019. https://www.politico.eu/article/trump-weighs-conditioning-foreign-aid-on-religious-freedom/.

Wootliff, Raoul. "Final Text of Jewish Nation-State Law, Approved by the Knesset Early on July 19." *Times of Israel*, July 19, 2018. https://www.timesofisrael.com/final-text-of-jewish-nation-state-bill-set-to-become-law/.

LITERATURE

Abdelhady, Dalia. *The Lebanese Diaspora: The Arab Immigrant Experience in Montreal, New York, and Paris*. New York: New York University Press, 2011.

Abousefian, Marie Rose. "Germany's Responsibility in the Armenian Genocide." 2015. https://www.academia.edu/25335289/Germanys_Responsibility_in_the_Armenian_Genocide.

Aly, Abdel Monem Said, and Manfred W. Wenner. "Modern Islamic Reform Movements: The Muslim Brotherhood in Contemporary Egypt." *Middle East Journal* 36, no. 3 (1982): 336–61. https://www.academia.edu/43467760/Modern_Islamic_Reform_Movement_The_Muslim_Brotherhood_in_contemporary_Egypt.

Anderson, Benedict. *Imagined Communities: Reflections on the Origin and Spread of Nationalism*. Rev. ed. London: Verso, 2016.

Anscombe, Frederick F. *State, Faith, and Nation in Ottoman and Post-Ottoman Lands*. New York: Cambridge University Press, 2014.

Alvaredo, Facundo, and Thomas Piketty. "Measuring Top Incomes and Inequality in the Middle East: Data Limitations and

Illustration with the Case of Egypt." April 13, 2014. http://piketty
.pse.ens.fr/files/AlvaredoPiketty2014MiddleEast.pdf.

Arnove, Anthony, ed. *Iraq under Siege, Updated Edition: The Deadly Impact of Sanctions and War.* Rev. ed. Cambridge, Mass.: South End Press, 2003.

Azoury, Negib. *Le reveil de la nation arabe.* Repr. ed. Whitefish, Mont.: Kessinger, 2010.

Badr, Ḥabīb. "Mission to 'Nominal Christians': The Policy and Practice of American Board of Commissioners for Foreign Missions and Its Missionaries Concerning Eastern Churches Which Led to the Organization of a Protestant Church in Beirut (1819–1848)." PhD diss., Princeton Theological Seminary, Princeton, N.J., 1992.

Beehner, Lionel. "The Effects of 'Youth Bulge' on Civil Conflicts." Council on Foreign Relations, 2007. https://web.archive.org/web/20130527020909/http://www.cfr.org/society-and-culture/effects-youth-bulge-civil-conflicts/p13093.

Brown, Nathan J., and Amr Hamzawy. *Between Religion and Politics.* Washington, D.C.: Carnegie Endowment for International Peace, 2010.

Bush, Luis. "The Challenge before Us." In *Proclaim Christ until He Comes: Calling the Whole Church to Take the Whole Gospel to the Whole World,* edited by J. D. Douglas, 58–62. Minneapolis: World Wide, 1990. https://web.archive.org/web/20110610230732/http://www.lausanne.org/documents/lau2docs/058.pdf.

Chatelard, Géraldine. "Migration from Iraq between the Gulf and the Iraq Wars (1990–2003): Historical and Sociospacial Dimensions." Centre on Migration, Policy and Society, 2009. https://www.academia.edu/182775/Migration_from_Iraq_between_the_Gulf_and_the_Iraq_Wars_1990-2003_Historical_and_Sociospacial_Dimensions.

Churchill, Charles Henry. *The Druzes and the Maronites under the Turkish Rule, from 1840 to 1860.* London: Bernard Quaritch, 1862. http://archive.org/details/druzesmaronitesu00churuoft.

Cohen, Arthur Allen. *The Myth of the Judeo-Christian Tradition, and Other Dissenting Essays.* New York: Schocken Books, 1971.

Commins, David. *The Wahhabi Mission and Saudi Arabia.* London: I. B. Tauris, 2006.

Courbage, Youssef, and Philippe Fargues. *Christians and Jews under Islam.* London: I. B. Tauris, 1996.

Daccache, Salim. "Catholic Missions in the Middle East." In *Christianity: A History in the Middle East*, edited by Habib Badr, 687–713. Beirut: World Council of Churches, 2005.

Dadrian, Vahakn N. *German Responsibility in the Armenian Genocide: A Review of the Historical Evidence of German Complicity*. 3rd ed. Watertown, Mass.: Blue Crane Books, 1996.

———. *The History of the Armenian Genocide: Ethnic Conflict from the Balkans to Anatolia to the Caucasus*. New York: Berghahn Books, 2003.

Darwish, Mahmoud. *Unfortunately, It Was Paradise: Selected Poems*. Translated and edited by Sinan Antoon and Carolyn Forché. Berkeley: University of California Press, 2003, 2013.

Davison, Roderic H. *Reform in the Ottoman Empire, 1856–1876*. Repr. ed. Princeton, N.J.: Princeton University Press, 2016.

Donabed, Sargon. *Reforging a Forgotten History: Iraq and the Assyrians in the Twentieth Century*. Repr. ed. Edinburgh: Edinburgh University Press, 2016.

Doorn-Harder, Nelly van. "Kyrillos VI (1902–1971): Planner, Patriarch and Saint." In *Between Desert and City: The Coptic Orthodox Church Today*, edited by Nelly van Doorn-Harder, 231–43. Repr. ed. Eugene, Ore.: Wipf & Stock, 2012.

———. "Signposts to Biography: Pope Shenouda III." In *Between Desert and City: The Coptic Orthodox Church Today*, edited by Nelly van Doorn-Harder, 244–54. Repr. ed. Eugene, Ore.: Wipf & Stock, 2012.

Eleftheriadou, Marina. "Christian Militias in Syria and Iraq: Beyond the Neutrality/Passivity Debate." *Middle East Bulletin* 28 (2015): 13–19. https://www.academia.edu/13467603/Christian_militias _in_Syria_and_Iraq_beyond_the_neutrality_passivity_debate.

Erakat, Noura. "Whiteness as Property in Israel: Revival, Rehabilitation, and Removal." *Harvard Journal of Ethnic and Racial Justice* 69 (2015): 69–104. https://www.academia.edu/33926126/ Whiteness_as_Property_in_Israel_Revival_Rehabilitation _and_Removal.

Farah, Ceasar E. *The Politics of Interventionism in Ottoman Lebanon, 1830–1861*. London: I. B. Tauris, 2000.

Fawaz, Leila Tarazi. *Merchants and Migrants in Nineteenth-Century Beirut*. Cambridge, Mass.: Harvard University Press, 2000.

———. *An Occasion for War: Civil Conflict in Lebanon and Damascus in 1860*. Berkeley: University of California Press, 1995.

Forman, Geremy, and Alexandre (Sandy) Kedar. "From Arab Land to 'Israel Lands': The Legal Dispossession of the Palestinians Displaced by Israel in the Wake of 1948." *Environment and Planning D: Society and Space* 22, no. 6 (2004): 809–30. https://doi.org/10.1068/d402.

Fox, Jonathan. *A World Survey of Religion and the State.* Cambridge: Cambridge University Press, 2008.

Frampton, Martyn. *The Muslim Brotherhood and the West: A History of Enmity and Engagement.* Cambridge, Mass.: Belknap Press, 2018.

Frantzman, Seth J., Benjamin W. Glueckstadt, and Ruth Kark. "The Anglican Church in Palestine and Israel: Colonialism, Arabization and Land Ownership." *Middle Eastern Studies* 47, no. 1 (2011): 101–26. https://doi.org/10.1080/00263201003590482.

Frantzman, Seth J., and Ruth Kark. "The Catholic Church in Palestine/Israel: Real Estate in Terra Sancta." *Middle Eastern Studies* 50, no. 3 (2014): 370–96. https://doi.org/10.1080/00263206.2013.871266.

Frary, Lucien J., and Mara Kozelsky, eds. *Russian-Ottoman Borderlands: The Eastern Question Reconsidered.* Madison: University of Wisconsin Press, 2014.

Freas, Erik. *Muslim-Christian Relations in Late-Ottoman Palestine: Where Nationalism and Religion Intersect.* New York: Palgrave Macmillan, 2016.

From the Nile to the Euphrates: The Call of Faith and Citizenship. Bethlehem: Diyar, 2015.

Gaunt, David. *Massacres, Resistance, Protectors: Muslim-Christian Relations in Eastern Anatolia during World War I.* Piscataway, N.J.: Gorgias Press, 2006.

Gaunt, David, Naures Atto, and Soner O. Barthoma, eds. *Let Them Not Return: Sayfo—the Genocide against the Assyrian, Syriac, and Chaldean Christians in the Ottoman Empire.* New York: Berghahn Books, 2018.

Graubard, Stephen R., and Richard G. Hovannisian, eds. *The Armenian Genocide in Perspective.* New York: Routledge, 2017.

Greenberg, Ela. *Preparing the Mothers of Tomorrow: Education and Islam in Mandate Palestine.* Austin: University of Texas Press, 2010.

Guirguis, Magdi, and Michael Shelley. *The Emergence of the Modern Coptic Papacy.* Vol. 3 of *The Popes of Egypt.* Cairo: American University in Cairo Press, 2011.

Gunner, Goran, and Robert O. Smith, eds. *Comprehending Christian Zionism: Perspectives in Comparison*. Minneapolis: Fortress, 2014.

Gurr, Ted Robert. *Why Men Rebel*. New York: Routledge, 2011.

Gust, Wolfgang, ed. *The Armenian Genocide: Evidence from the German Foreign Office Archives, 1915–1916*. New York: Berghahn Books, 2013.

Haddad, Yvonne, and Rahel Fischbach. "Interfaith Dialogue in Lebanon: Between a Power Balancing Act and Theological Encounters." *Islam and Christian Muslim Relations* 26, no. 4 (2015): 423–42. https://www.academia.edu/17740013/Interfaith_Dialogue_in _Lebanon.

Hafez, Mohammed M., and Marc-André Walther. "Hamas: Between Pragmatism and Radicalism." In *Routledge Handbook of Political Islam*. New York: Routledge, 2011. https://www.academia.edu/ 11762479/Hamas_Between_Pragmatism_and_Radicalism.

Hanssen, Jens, Hicham Safieddine, and Ussama Samir Makdisi. *The Clarion of Syria: A Patriot's Call against the Civil War of 1860*. Oakland: University of California Press, 2019.

Harris, William. *Lebanon: A History, 600–2011*. Repr. ed. Oxford: Oxford University Press, 2014.

Hasan, S. S. *Christians versus Muslims in Modern Egypt: The Century-Long Struggle for Coptic Equality*. Oxford: Oxford University Press, 2003.

Haynes, Stephen R. "Christian Holocaust Theology: A Critical Reassessment." *Journal of the American Academy of Religion* 62, no. 2 (1994): 553–85.

Henley, Alexander D. M. "Politics of a Church at War: Maronite Catholicism in the Lebanese Civil War." *Mediterranean Politics* 13, no. 3 (2008): 353–69.

Herzl, Theodor. *The Jewish State: An Attempt at a Modern Solution of the Jewish Question*. Edited by Jacob de Haas. Translated by Sylvie d'Avigdor. Repr. ed. Whithorn, UK: Anodos Books, 2018.

Hodder, Edwin. *The Life and Work of the Seventh Earl of Shaftesbury, K.G.* Vol. 2. London: Cassell, 1886.

Hopwood, Derek. *The Russian Presence in Syria & Palestine 1843–1914*. Oxford: Clarendon, 1969.

Hourani, Albert, and Nadim Shehadi. *The Lebanese in the World: A Century of Emigration*. London: Centre for Lebanese Studies; I. B. Tauris, 1992.

Hubers, John. *I Am a Pilgrim, a Traveler, a Stranger: Exploring the Life and Mind of the First American Missionary to the Middle East, the Rev. Pliny Fisk.* Eugene, Ore.: Pickwick, 2016.

Ikehata, Fukiko. "Interfaith Dialogue in Jordan: Bridging the Gap between Christianity and Islam." *Mediterranean Review* 10, no. 2 (2017): 63–82. https://www.academia.edu/36363252/Interfaith_Dialogue_in_Jordan_Bridging_the_Gap_between_Christianity_and_Islam.

Jok, Jok Madut. *Sudan: Race, Religion, and Violence.* Rev. ed. Oxford: Oneworld, 2015.

Kassis, Rifat Odeh, Rania Al Qass Collings, and Mitri Raheb, eds. *Palestinian Christians in the West Bank: Facts, Figures and Trends.* Bethlehem: CreateSpace, 2012.

Katz, Itamar, and Ruth Kark. "The Church and Landed Property: The Greek Orthodox Patriarchate of Jerusalem." *Middle Eastern Studies* 43, no. 3 (2007): 383–408. https://doi.org/10.1080/00263200701245969.

Kawerau, Peter. *Amerika und die orientalischen Kirchen: Ursprung und Anfang der amerikanischen Mission unter den Nationalkirchen Westasiens.* Arbeiten Zur Kirchengeschichte 31. Bethlehem: Diyar, 2017.

Kévorkian, Raymond. *The Armenian Genocide: A Complete History.* London: I. B. Tauris, 2011.

Khalaf, Samir. *Protestant Missionaries in the Levant: Ungodly Puritans, 1820–1860.* New York: Routledge, 2017.

Khalidi, Rashid. *British Policy towards Syria & Palestine, 1906–1914: A Study of the Antecedents of the Hussein-the [sic] McMahon Correspondence, the Sykes-Picot Agreement, and the Balfour Declaration.* London: Ithaca Press, 1980.

———. *The Hundred Years' War on Palestine: A History of Settler Colonialism and Resistance, 1917–2017.* New York: Metropolitan Books, 2020.

Kickel, Walter. *Das gelobte Land: Die religiöse Bedeutung des Staates Israel in jüdischer und christlicher Sicht.* Munich: Kösel, 1984.

Kildani, Hanna. *Modern Christianity in the Holy Land.* Bloomington, Ind.: AuthorHouse, 2010.

Knapp, Andreas. *The Last Christians: Stories of Persecution, Flight, and Resilience in the Middle East.* Translated by Sharon Howe. Walden: Plough, 2017.

Kymlicka, Will, and Eva Pföstl, eds. *Minority Politics in the Middle East and North Africa: The Prospects for Transformative Change.* New York: Routledge, 2016.

Lefevre, Raphael. *Ashes of Hama: The Muslim Brotherhood in Syria.* New York: Oxford University Press, 2013.

Levine, Mark. *Overthrowing Geography: Jaffa, Tel Aviv, and the Struggle for Palestine, 1880–1948.* Berkeley: University of California Press, 2005.

Lewis, Donald M. *The Origins of Christian Zionism: Lord Shaftesbury and Evangelical Support for a Jewish Homeland.* Repr. ed. New York: Cambridge University Press, 2014.

Lindsey, Hal, and Carole C. Carlson. *The Late Great Planet Earth.* Grand Rapids: Zondervan Academic, 1970.

Makari, Peter E. *Conflict and Cooperation: Christian-Muslim Relations in Contemporary Egypt.* Syracuse, N.Y.: Syracuse University Press, 2007.

Makdisi, Ussama. *Age of Coexistence: The Ecumenical Frame and the Making of the Modern Arab World.* Oakland: University of California Press, 2019.

———. *Artillery of Heaven: American Missionaries and the Failed Conversion of the Middle East.* Ithaca, N.Y.: Cornell University Press, 2009.

———. *The Culture of Sectarianism.* Berkeley: University of California Press, 2000.

Mansour, Johnny. *Arab Christians in Israel: Facts, Figures and Trends.* Bethlehem: Diyar, 2012.

———. *A New Vision of the Life and Works of Bishop Gregorios Hajjar.* New ed. Haifa: Al-Hakeem 2013.

Marlin, George J. *Christian Persecutions in the Middle East: A 21st Century Tragedy.* South Bend, Ind.: St. Augustine's Press, 2015.

Masalha, Nur. *The Zionist Bible: Biblical Precedent, Colonialism and the Erasure of Memory.* New York: Routledge, 2014.

Masters, Bruce. *The Arabs of the Ottoman Empire, 1516–1918: A Social and Cultural History.* Cambridge: Cambridge University Press, 2013.

———. *Christians and Jews in the Ottoman Arab World: The Roots of Sectarianism.* Rev. ed. Cambridge: Cambridge University Press, 2004.

Matossian, Bedross Der. "Explaining the Unexplainable: Recent Trends in the Armenian Genocide Historiography." *Journal of Levantine Studies* 5, no. 2 (2015): 143–66. https://www.academia.edu/26383605/Bedross_Der_Matossian_Explaining_the

_Unexplainable_Recent_Trends_in_the_Armenian_Genocide
_Historiography_in_Journal_of_Levantine_Studies_Vol_5
_No_2_Winter_2015_pp_143_166.

May, Melanie. *Jerusalem Testament: Palestinian Christians Speak, 1988–2008*. Grand Rapids: Eerdmans, 2010.

McAlister, Melani. "The Politics of Persecution." *Middle East Report* 249 (2008). https://merip.org/2008/12/the-politics-of-persecution/.

McCallum, Fiona, John Anderson, and Raymond Hinnebusch. *Christian Religious Leadership in the Middle East: The Political Role of Patriarch*. Lewiston, N.Y.: Edwin Mellen, 2010.

Mearsheimer, John J., and Stephen M. Walt. *The Israel Lobby and U.S. Foreign Policy*. New York: FSG Adult, 2008.

Momani, Bessma. *Arab Dawn: Arab Youth and the Demographic Dividend They Will Bring*. Toronto: University of Toronto Press, 2015.

Morris, Benny. "Operation Hiram Revisited: A Correction." *Journal of Palestine Studies* 28, no. 2 (1999): 68–76.

Morris, Benny, and Dror Ze'evi. *The Thirty-Year Genocide: Turkey's Destruction of Its Christian Minorities, 1894–1924*. Cambridge, Mass.: Harvard University Press, 2019.

Mujais, Salim. *The Syrian Social Nationalist Party: Its Ideology and History*. London: Black House, 2019.

Musallam, A. Adnan. "The Formative Stages of Palestinian Arab Immigration to Latin America and Immigrants' Quest for Return and for the Palestinian Citizenship in the Early 1920's." In *Latin American with Palestinian Roots*, edited by Viola Raheb, 15–24. Bethlehem: Diyar, 2012.

Naff, Alixa. *Becoming American: The Early Arab Immigrant Experience*. M.E.R.I. Special Studies. Carbondale: Southern Illinois University Press, 1993.

New, David S. *Holy War: The Rise of Militant Christian, Jewish and Islamic Fundamentalism*. Jefferson, N.C.: McFarland, 2001.

Norris, Jacob. *Land of Progress: Palestine in the Age of Colonial Development, 1905–1948*. Oxford: Oxford University Press, 2013.

O'Mahony, Anthony. *The Christian Communities of Jerusalem and the Holy Land: Studies in History, Religion and Politics*. Cardiff: University of Wales Press, 2003.

O'Mahony, Anthony, and Emma Loosley. *Eastern Christianity in the Modern Middle East*. Culture and Civilisation in the Middle East 20. New York: Routledge, 2010.

Pal, Jeremy S., and Elfatih A. B. Eltahir. "Future Temperature in Southwest Asia Projected to Exceed a Threshold for Human Adaptability." *Nature Climate Change* 6, no. 2 (2016): 197–200. https://doi.org/10.1038/nclimate2833.

Papastathis, Konstantinos, and Ruth Kark. "Colonialism and Religious Power Politics: The Question of New Regulations within the Orthodox Church of Jerusalem during the British Mandate." *Middle Eastern Studies* 50, no. 4 (2014): 589–605.

Pappé, Ilan. *The Ethnic Cleansing of Palestine*. 2nd ed. London: Oneworld, 2007.

———. *The Modern Middle East: A Social and Cultural History*. 3rd ed. New York: Routledge, 2014.

Raheb, Mitri. "Christianity in the Middle East, 1799–1917." In *History of Global Christianity*, vol. 2, edited by Jens Holger Schjørring and Norman Hjelm, 247–66. Boston: Brill, 2018.

———. "Christianity in the Middle East, 1917–2017." In *History of Global Christianity*, vol. 3, edited by Jens Holger Schjørring, Norman Hjelm, and Kevin Ward, 375–95. Boston: Brill, 2018.

———, ed. *Diaspora and Identity: The Case of Palestine*. Bethlehem: Diyar, 2017.

———. "Displacement Theopolitics." In *The Invention of History: A Century of Interplay between Theology and Politics in Palestine*, edited by Mitri Raheb, 9–32. Bethlehem: Diyar, 2011.

———. *Faith in the Face of Empire: The Bible through Palestinian Eyes*. Maryknoll, N.Y.: Orbis, 2014.

———, ed. *God's Reign and People's Rule: Constitution, Religion, and Identity in Palestine*. Berlin: AphorismA, 2009.

———, ed. *Jerusalem: Religious, National and International Dimensions*. Bethlehem: Diyar, 2019.

———, ed. *Middle Eastern Women: The Intersection of Law, Culture and Religion*. Bethlehem: Diyar, 2020.

———. "Palestinian Christian Reflections on Christian Zionism." In *Comprehending Christian Zionism: Perspectives in Comparison*, edited by Goran Gunner and Robert O. Smith, 191–98. Minneapolis: Fortress, 2014.

———. "Palestinian Christians in Modern History: Between Migration and Displacement." In *Palestinian Christians: Emigration, Displacement and Diaspora*, edited by Mitri Raheb, 9–28. Bethlehem: Diyar, 2017.

———. "Protestants." In *Christianity in North Africa & West Asia*, edited by Kenneth Ross, Mariz Tadros, and Todd Johnson, 259–70. Peabody, Mass.: Hendrickson, 2020.

———. *Das reformatorische Erbe unter den Palästinensern: Zur Entstehung der Evangelisch-Lutherischen Kirche in Jordanien*. Vol. 11. Reihe: Die Lutherische Kirche. Geschichte und Gestalten. Gütersloh: Gütersloher Verlagshaus, Gerd Mohn, 1990.

———. *Sailing through Troubled Waters: Christianity in the Middle East*. Bethlehem: Diyar, 2013.

———, ed. *Shifting Identities: Changes in the Social, Political, and Religious Structures in the Arab World*. Bethlehem: Diyar, 2016.

———. "Shifting Identities: The History of Christianity in the Modern Middle East." In *Shifting Identities: Changes in the Social, Political, and Religious Structures in the Arab World*, edited by Mitri Raheb, 9–38. Bethlehem: Diyar, 2016.

Raheb, Mitri, and Suzanne Watts Henderson. *The Cross in Contexts: Suffering and Redemption in Palestine*. Maryknoll, N.Y.: Orbis, 2017.

Raheb, Viola. "Sisters and Brothers in the Diaspora: Palestinian Christians in Latin America." In *Latin American with Palestinian Roots*, ed. Viola Raheb, 9–14. Bethlehem: Diyar, 2012.

Reimer, Michael J. *Colonial Bridgehead: Government and Society in Alexandria, 1807–1882*. Repr. ed. London: Routledge, 2019.

Robson, Laura. *Colonialism and Christianity in Mandate Palestine*. Repr. ed. Austin: University of Texas Press, 2012.

———. *States of Separation: Transfer, Partition, and the Making of the Modern Middle East*. Oakland: University of California Press, 2017.

Robson, Laura, ed. *Minorities and the Modern Arab World: New Perspectives*. Repr. ed. Syracuse, N.Y.: Syracuse University Press, 2016.

Roszkiewicz, J., Karina Walinowicz, Marcin Rau, and Olaf Szczypiński. *Persecution of Christians: Time to React to Genocide*. Warsaw: Ordo Iuris Institute for Legal Culture, 2017. https://www.academia.edu/33778713/Persecution_of_Christians_Time_to_React_to_Genocide.

Rubin, Lawrence. "Politics, Religion and Ideology: The Rise of Official Islam in Jordan." *Politics, Religion & Ideology* 14, no. 1 (2013): 59–74. https://www.academia.edu/23847994/Politics_Religion_and_Ideology_The_Rise_of_Official_Islam_in_Jordan.

Rychlak, Ronald J., and Jane F. Adolphe, eds. *The Persecution and Genocide of Christians in the Middle East: Prevention, Prohibition, & Prosecution.* Kettering, Ohio: Angelico Press, 2017.

Sagi, Avi, and Dov Schwartz. *Religious Zionism and the Six Day War: From Realism to Messianism.* London: Routledge, 2018.

Said, Edward W. *Orientalism.* New York: Vintage, 1979.

Salloum, Saad. *At Crossroads: Iraqi Minorities after ISIS.* N.p.: Masarat for Cultural and Media Development, n.d. Accessed July 5, 2020. https://www.academia.edu/33552150/Iraqi_Minorities_After _ISIS.pdf.

Sand, Shlomo. *The Invention of the Jewish People.* Translated by Yael Lotan. London: Verso, 2010.

Shabbah, Michel. *Faithful Witness: On Reconciliation and Peace in the Holy Land.* New York: New City Press, 2008.

Sharkey, Heather J. *American Evangelicals in Egypt: Missionary Encounters in an Age of Empire.* Repr. ed. Princeton, N.J.: Princeton University Press, 2015.

———. *A History of Muslims, Christians, and Jews in the Middle East.* Cambridge: Cambridge University Press, 2017.

Sinno, Abdel-Raouf. *Deutsche Interessen in Syrien und Palästina 1841–1898: Aktivitäten religiöser Institutionen, wirtschaftliche und politische Einflüsse.* Berlin: Baalbek Verlag, 1982.

Siriani, Razek. "Syria." In *Christianity in North Africa and West Asia,* edited by Kenneth R. Ross, Mariz Tadros, and Todd M. Johnson, 102–13. Edinburgh: Edinburgh University Press, 2018.

Sizer, Stephen, and David G. Peterson. *Christian Zionism: Road-Map to Armageddon?* IVP/UK ed. Leicester: IVP Academic, 2006.

Smith, Robert O. *More Desired Than Our Owne Salvation: The Roots of Christian Zionism.* New York: Oxford University Press, 2013.

Stegagno, Carlotta. "The Foundation of the Ba'th Party: The Ideology of Michel 'Aflaq." Accessed November 12, 2020. https://www .academia.edu/16561697/The_foundation_of_the_Bath_Party _the_ideology_of_Michel_Aflaq.

Suny, Ronald Grigor, Fatma Muge Gocek, and Norman M. Naimark, eds. *A Question of Genocide: Armenians and Turks at the End of the Ottoman Empire.* Oxford: Oxford University Press, 2011.

Szanto, Edith. "Inter-religious Dialogue in Syria: Politics, Ethics and Miscommunication." *Political Theology* 9, no. 1 (2008): 93–113. https://www.academia.edu/465177/Inter-Religious_Dialogue _in_Syria_Politics_Ethics_and_Miscommunication.

Tabar, Paul. "Lebanon: A Country of Emigration and Immigration." https://www.academia.edu/31369352/Lebanon_A_Country_of _Emigration_and_Immigration.

Tejirian, Eleanor, and Reeva Spector Simon. *Conflict, Conquest, and Conversion: Two Thousand Years of Christian Missions in the Middle East*. Repr. ed. New York: Columbia University Press, 2014.

Tibawi, A. L. *American Interests in Syria 1800–1901*. Oxford: Oxford University Press, 1966.

——. *Arab Education in Mandatory Palestine: A Study of Three Decades of British Administration*. London: Luzac, 1956.

——. *British Interests in Palestine 1800–1901*. Oxford: Oxford University Press, 1961.

Wehrey, Frederic. *Sectarian Politics in the Gulf: From the Iraq War to the Arab Uprisings*. Repr. ed. New York: Columbia University Press, 2016.

White, Benjamin Thomas. *The Emergence of Minorities in the Middle East: The Politics of Community in French Mandate Syria*. Repr. ed. Edinburgh: Edinburgh University Press, 2012.

Wolf, Lucien. *Notes on the Diplomatic History of the Jewish Question: With Texts of Protocols, Treaty Stipulations and Other Public Acts and Official Documents*. London: Spottiswoode, 1919. http://archive.org/details/notesondiplomatioowolfuoft.

Zachs, Fruma. "Feminism for Men: A Note on Butrus al-Bustani's *Lecture on the Education of Women* (1849)." In *Butrus al-Bustani: Spirit of the Age*, edited by Adel Beshara, 113–30. Melbourne: Iphoenix, 2014. https://www.academia.edu/15885629/Feminism _for_Men_A_Note_on_Butrus_al-Bustanis_Lecture_on_the _Education_of_Women_1849_.

Zurcher, Erik Jan. "Young Turks, Ottoman Muslims and Turkish Nationalist Identity Politics 1908–1938." In *Ottoman Past and Today's Turkey*, edited by K. H. Karpat, 150–79. Leiden: Brill, 2000. https://www.academia.edu/5726070/Young_Turks_Ottoman _Muslims_and_Turkish_Nationalists_Identity_Politics_1908 -1938.

INDEX

Italicized page numbers indicate key passages.

187

46–48, 51, 53, 57, 60–61, *65–70*, 76, 84, 130, 149–50; era, 3; Rule, 5, 9, 65–66, 73, 75

Pahlavi dynasty, 116

Pakistan, 87, 149

Palestine, 1, 3–6, 9, 12, 14, 18–20, 22–23, 27–28, 30–31, 51, 54–55, *57–64*, 66, 69, 73–74, 76, 78–81, 83–84, 87–89, 91–92, 94–95, 99, 105–6, 108–10, 123–24, 129–31, 133, 150; Holy Land, 10, 17, 20–22, 28, 31, 61, 88, 95, 111, 123; Palestinian(s), 1–2, 4, 6, 48–49, 64, 66, 76, 79, 88–89, 91–95, 97, 103, 105–6, 108–10, 112, 115, 120, 123–24, 131, 149–51, 153; Palestinian independence, 2–3, 79; *see also* diaspora, Palestinian

Palestine Kairos Document, 124

Palestinian Authority, 2

Palestinian Evangelical Congregation, 81

Palestinian Liberation Organization (PLO), 2, 105, 109–10

"The Palestinian Question as a Challenge to Christian Faith," 109

Palm Sunday, 146

pan-Arabism, 3, 6, 75, *98–103*, 105, 108–10, 121–22

pan-Islamism, 3, 83; pan-Islamic organization(s), 83

pan-Slavic movement, 30

pan-Syrian, 75–76

papacy: *see* pope

Pappe, Ilan, 102

Paris: *see* France, Paris

Paris Peace Conference, 84

Parsons, Levi, 19, 23

partition, 36–37, 78, 87; *see also* UN Partition 1947

pasha(s), 82

Pasha, Ibrahim, 14, 20, 27, 34–35, 42, 47, 58, 61

Pasha, Mahmud Kamil, 70

Pasha, Muhammad Ali, 13

patriarch(s), 11, 26–29, 55, 80–81,

101, 112–13, 124; patriarchate, 10, 55, 80; *see also* Arida, Patriarch; Athenagoras (ecumenical patriarch of Constantinople); Eastern Catholic Churches; Ecumenical Patriarchate of Constantinople; Greek Orthodox patriarchates; Hoayek, Elias; Hubaysh, Yusuf; Khreish, Maronite patriarch; Maronite, patriarch; Mazlum, Maximus; Rai, Maronite patriarch; Sabbah, Michel; Sfeir, Nasrallah; Valerga, Patriarch; Yazigi, Antiochian Orthodox patriarch

patriot(s), 42; patriotism, 44

Paul VI, Pope, 101; *see also* pope

peace, 38, 76, 110, 125–26, 131, 152, 154: peace movement, 123; *see also* Camp David Peace Treaty; Paris Peace Conference; Versailles Peace Conference

Peel Commission, 78

Pelikan pens, 82

Pence, Vice President, 145–48

Pen League, 49

persecution, 1, 7, 25–27, 34, 37, 71, 120, 122, 153–54; Christian, vii, 1–4, 33, 44, 46, 143–49, 151, 155–56

Persia: Holy See in, 28

Persian Gulf: *see* Gulf, Persian

Petit Liban, 75; *see also* Grand Liban

petrodollar(s), 6, 108, 113, *117*, 119, 121, 127

Pew Research Center, 136

Phalangist Party, 112

Philadelphia Centennial Exposition, 48

pilgrim, 31; pilgrimage, 31, 111

Pius IX, Pope, 29; *see also* pope

Pius XII, Pope, 93; *see also* pope

PLO: *see* Palestinian Liberation Organization

pluralism, 30, 103, 148, 152–53

Pontifical Mission for Palestine, 93

pope, 10, 26–27, 29–30, 50, 93, 101–2, 110–12, 124, 126; defeat